Football School

Name: ........................................

Class: ........................................

Coaches: ..............................

Kickito Ergo Sum

To Harry M. – A.B.

To ABBC, with love – B.L.

For my mum – S.G.

First published 2020 by Walker Books Ltd
87 Vauxhall Walk, London SE11 5HJ

2 4 6 8 10 9 7 5 3 1



This book has been typeset in Gill Sans and WB Spike

Printed and bound by CPI Group (UK) Ltd, Croydon CR0 4YY



British Library Cataloguing in Publication Data:
a catalogue record for this book is available from the British Library

ISBN 978-1-4063-8665-3

WALKER BOOKS

FSC www.fsc.org MIX Paper from responsible sources FSC® C020471

www.walker.co.uk

www.footballschool.co

# FOOTBALL SCHOOL

# EPIC HEROES

50 TRUE TALES THAT SHOOK THE WORLD

ALEX BELLOS & BEN LYTTLETON

Illustrated by Spike Gerrell

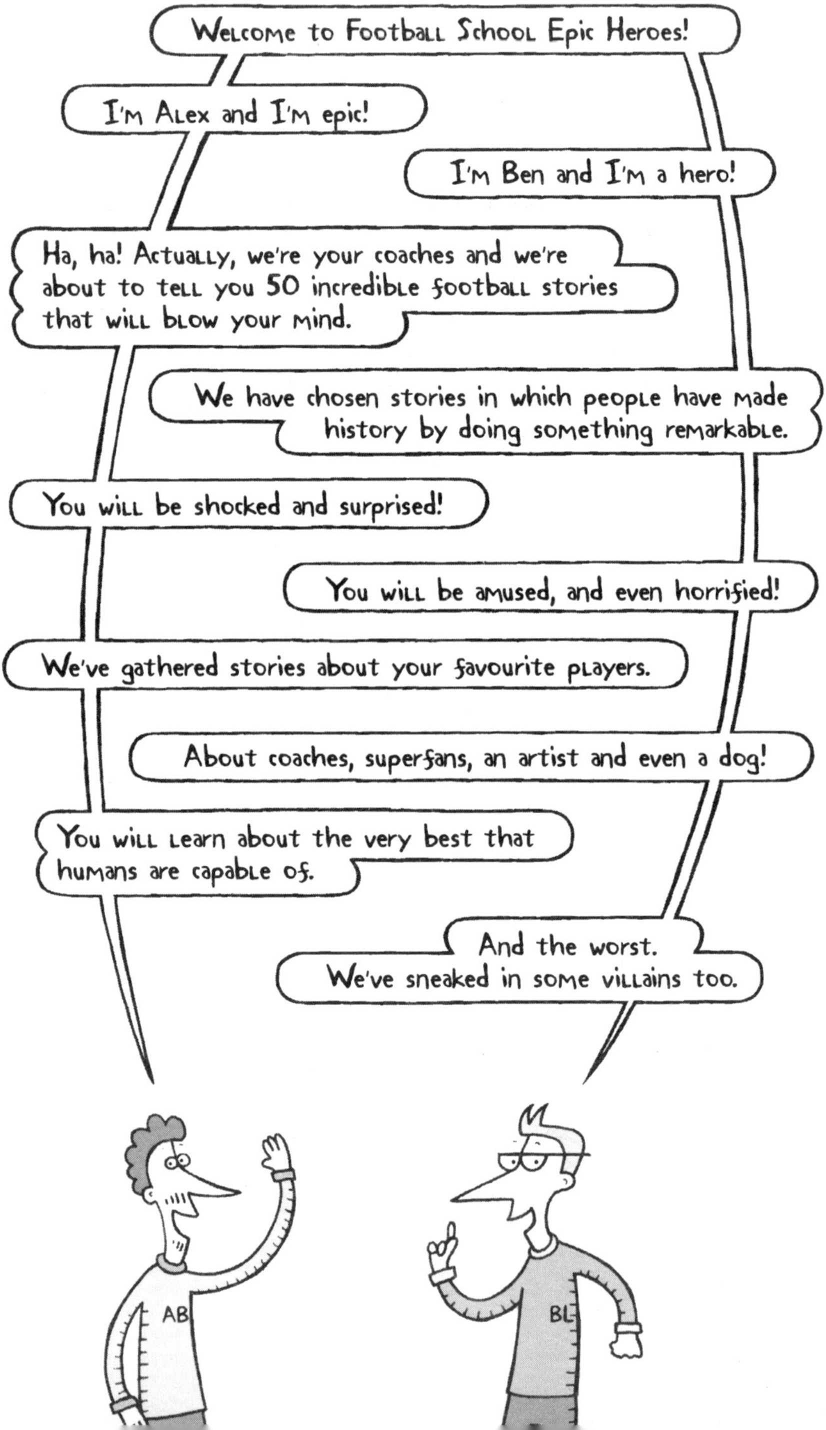
Welcome to Football School Epic Heroes!
I'm Alex and I'm epic!
I'm Ben and I'm a hero!
Ha, ha! Actually, we're your coaches and we're about to tell you 50 incredible football stories that will blow your mind.
We have chosen stories in which people have made history by doing something remarkable.
You will be shocked and surprised!
You will be amused, and even horrified!
We've gathered stories about your favourite players.
About coaches, superfans, an artist and even a dog!
You will learn about the very best that humans are capable of.
And the worst. We've sneaked in some villains too.
AB
BL

We'll travel across the world, from Argentina to Zambia, and from Britain to Bhutan.
Boot! On!
And we'll hear gripping and intriguing stories about clubs, such as Arsenal, Liverpool, Spurs and Real Madrid.
Olé! Olé!
The stories are so thrilling we have made them front page news. In our tabloid newspaper Goal, you will find the most dramatic and outrageous tales.
In the broadsheet newspaper Football Times, you'll read about some amazing moments from history.
In our magazine Football, we have profiles of players.
And at backofthenet.co.uk we've got reports of intriguing derring-do.
READ ALL ABOUT IT!
SCROLL DOWN AND SHARE!
And once you've read all the 50 stories, we have a quiz to test you on everything you have learned.
Let's go!
AB
BL

FOOTBALL
MAGAZINE
London, 2020
PEN PALS
The inside story of
Football School
BL
AB

The first story in this book is the epic tale of Football School. Alex and Ben are best friends who wanted to work together. As they both love football, they decided to write a series of books that they wished they had read when they were younger. The pair also love silly jokes so were determined to make Football School as funny as possible for their readers. The result was the Football School series; and you are holding one of their books right now.

Just like everyone else in this book, the two pals have had their own epic football moments. Alex once joined a game of football in Brazil that was being played on a mud pitch beside the Amazon river at low tide. It was so slippery he fell over before he had even touched the ball!

Ben was once mistaken for a professional footballer and asked to sign autographs for a group of fans. He decided to play along and spent ages signing his name. It was the closest he ever came to life as a top footballer!

Working together on Football School has also made Alex and Ben closer friends. They say the biggest lesson they have learned from writing together is that we are all stronger if we work with each other. These two are team-mates on and off the page!

**EPIK FACT**

Behind every great writing team is a great artist. Football School would be nothing without the series illustrator Spike Gerrell and his hilarious spiky drawings. You can even rearrange his name and come up with the letters: EPIK. What a hero!

# CONTENTS

FOOTBALL
MAGAZINE
Brazil, 1948
TOP DOG
Lucky hound
wins the league

We all know how a star player can transform the fortunes of a team. But what about a star pooch? Biriba is one of the most famous figures in the history of Brazilian club Botafogo. He was no dogged defender. He was an actual dog!

To Carlito Rocha, Botafogo's president, the fact that Biriba had four legs and a tail was no impediment to his being a crucial part of the team. Indeed, during the 1948 Rio de Janeiro championship, Biriba was on the payroll. It was the president's sincere belief that the club's success was dog-dependent.

Biriba was a black and white mongrel who had been found in the street by a former Botafogo defender called Macaé. No one quite knows how the dog first made his mark. One story has it that Macaé took Biriba to watch Botafogo's reserves. During one of the team's attacks, the ball went flying towards the opposition goal. So did the mischievous mutt, who ran onto the pitch, distracted the keeper, and the ball went in. The referee let the goal stand.

Another story has it that Macaé took the pooch to a match but they got separated entering the stadium. When Botafogo scored, however, Biriba appeared from nowhere, running onto the pitch to celebrate with the players.

Whichever of these two stories is correct, what is not in doubt is that Rocha decided that the dog was to become the club's mascot. It made sense, at least in terms of the team colours. Botafogo, one of Rio de Janeiro's biggest clubs, play in black and white, and the dog was black and white too.

But Rocha was very superstitious and Biriba became more than just a mascot. Rocha thought Biriba was necessary for the team to have good fortune, so the dog became the team's twelfth man. Not only did Biriba attend every game, but Rocha paid him the same bonuses as the first team players and insisted that the team chef cooked him the best cuts of meat. When Botafogo were due to travel by rail to a game, a player was booted off the train to make space for the dog.

Everything Biriba did was seen as important. Once, before a game, he peed on a player's leg. Rocha thought this was a good omen, so he insisted that before every further match Biriba must pee on the same leg.

He even helped the team's strategy. During games, the dog would usually sit with the team in the dugout. Occasionally he would be let loose onto the pitch to cool a game down. The referee would have to stop the play, by which time Botafogo had regained the psychological advantage.

With Biriba's help, Botafogo were doing well in the Rio championship, and the other sides decided to take action against the lucky hound. The dog was refused entrance to the stadium of a rival team. Rocha kicked up a fuss, and he was eventually allowed to watch the game with Biriba sitting on his lap.

Botafogo reached the play-off that would decide the title. Rocha heard that the opposing team had a plan to poison Biriba, so he ordered Macaé to sleep with the dog at the club's headquarters, and to taste the dog's food before he ate it to make sure it hadn't been tampered with! The dog (and Macaé) were unharmed.

Did Biriba bring the team good luck or not? Rocha certainly thought so, because Botafogo won the championship in 1948. Biriba was placed in front of the players for the team photo. He was given a gold collar with the club badge and even served champagne in a silver-plated dish. Biriba, take a bow wow wow!

**EPIC FACTS**

Carlito Rocha introduced other superstitious practices he hoped would give Botafogo the edge:

- The curtains at the club were tied in knots, to symbolize tying up the opposition.
- The defenders had to put the name of the player they were marking in their boots, so they would be on top of them before the game.

THE FOOTBALL TIMES

SPECIAL EDITION France, 2020

# Olympique champions

## Lyon women win fourteen in a row

**Above: Olympique Lyonnais Féminin have won fourteen consecutive French league titles.**

No football team playing today has been as successful as Olympique Lyonnais Féminin. In fact, perhaps no sports team has ever been this successful. Lyon have won fourteen French league titles in a row. Fourteen! In a six-year period between 2014 and 2020, the team lost only one league game and had a goal difference of +588. That means over all the matches they played, they scored 588 goals more than they conceded. Imagine all those goal celebrations!

The team was set up in 2004 by Lyon owner, Jean-Michel Aulas. His strategy was simple: treat the players just like the men's team are treated. It sounds obvious, but not all clubs do this. Other clubs often look after their male players far better than they do their female players.

Many women's teams do not share training facilities with their male counterparts. At Lyon, the women's team share the same training ground as the men's team and have access to the same specialists to help with their recovery, nutrition, injury prevention and mental health. The training ground has images of the female players with their trophies – to inspire the whole club – and the two sets of players eat together after training.

They also travel to games in the same vehicles; either a private plane or a team bus. They call it the Lyon bus, not the men's or women's bus. Each player is given their own seat and has their name stitched into the headrest. There's no seat-stealing at Lyon!

This attitude of equality is one of the reasons why Lyon are so successful. When other players see how Lyon treat their female players, they want to join. So when Lyon wanted to sign USA stars like Hope Solo, Alex Morgan and Megan Rapinoe, they were happy to join the club as they knew they would improve as players. The same happened with England stars Lucy Bronze and Alex Greenwood. Success breeds more success.

## TABLE OF CHAMPIONS

Here is OLF's league record over recent seasons:

| Season | P | W | D | L | F | A | GD | Pts | Position |
|---|---|---|---|---|---|---|---|---|---|
| 2014–15 | 22 | 22 | 0 | 0 | 147 | 6 | 141 | 88* | 1st |
| 2015–16 | 21 | 19 | 2 | 0 | 114 | 3 | 111 | 82* | 1st |
| 2016–17 | 22 | 21 | 0 | 1 | 103 | 6 | 97 | 63 | 1st |
| 2017–18 | 21 | 20 | 1 | 0 | 98 | 5 | 93 | 61 | 1st |
| 2018–19 | 22 | 20 | 2 | 0 | 89 | 6 | 83 | 62 | 1st |
| 2019–20 | 16 | 14 | 2 | 0 | 67 | 4 | 63 | 44 | 1st** |

*The French women's league used to award four points for a win, but changed to three points for a win in 2016.
** Title awarded to OLF after season ended early due to coronavirus.

The challenge for Lyon is to sustain this record of excellence while other teams work hard to close the gap on them. Paris Saint-Germain are getting closer in the French league, while across Europe, teams in England, Spain and Germany are dreaming of Champions League glory. As Lyon continues to set an epic standard for women's football, they are pushing other teams to improve so they might, one day, beat them.

**EPIC FACT**

In the 2019 Champions League final, the biggest club match in European football, Lyon beat Barcelona 4–1 to win their fourth Champions League crown in a row. The Lyon team contained some of the world's best players. As well as 2018 Ballon D'Or winner Ada Hegerberg, and 2019 Ballon D'Or runner-up Lucy Bronze, it also contained the national team captains of France (Amandine Henry) Germany (Dzsenifer Marozsán) and Japan (Saki Kumagai). That team had an army of armbands!

The GOAL
London, 1995
CANTONA
7
CANTONA
CANTONA KICKS FAN
WORLD STUNNED BY KUNG-FU ATTACK

Eric Cantona, one of France's best strikers in the 1990s, combined creativity, power and goals. He was a charismatic person who played with a swagger, and fans loved his style. But when it came to his most famous kick, the ball was nowhere in sight.

Cantona had just been sent off for Manchester United in an important Premier League game against Crystal Palace and was walking past the fans towards the dressing room. As he made his way along the touchline, one Palace fan ran from his seat eleven rows back to the front of the stand and shouted something at Cantona.

Whatever the fan had said made Cantona snap. He jumped feet first over the advertising hoarding and landed a kung-fu kick on the fan's midriff. He then tried to punch the fan before he was pulled away and escorted to the dressing room by United's stunned kit-man. The incident had lasted no more than 90 seconds but it was shocking. This attacker had attacked a fan!

The news spread and the TV footage appalled the nation. What kind of role model behaved like this? What had provoked Cantona into such violent and unexpected behaviour?

Cantona was a genius on the football pitch. He could score goals out of nothing and had helped his previous clubs Marseille and Leeds United both win league titles. He also had a short fuse and a quick temper – especially if he felt he had been wronged. He once threw the ball in disgust at a French referee and swore at the committee who were deciding on his punishment – so they doubled it!

As a result of his kung-fu kick, Cantona was banned from playing for nine months. He refused to apologize, which wasn't a surprise to those who knew him. Instead, he gave a puzzling statement that fans are still trying to decipher to this day: "When the seagulls follow the trawler, it's because they think sardines will be thrown into the sea." Do you have any idea what that might mean?!

### WHAT WAS THE SCORE AGAIN?

Years later, some of the Crystal Palace players who were on the pitch when Cantona kicked the Palace fan were asked about the match. Many of them had no memory of the final score. Two Palace players thought they had won; another that they had lost. In fact, the score ended 1–1. It was as if the shock had obliterated their memories!

One witness claimed that the fan had shouted racist abuse at Cantona, which had upset him and made him angry. People began to understand Cantona's reaction, even though everyone agreed he was still wrong to resort to violence. Cantona said that on any other day, he would have ignored the abusive comments, but on that day, he reacted.

Behind the scenes, United coach Sir Alex Ferguson gave Cantona his full support and helped him stay calm. Cantona returned to United when his ban was up, and played better than ever. The kung-fu kick was a turning point in his career. He was a calmer figure and was never sent off again. He inspired United to the next two Premier League titles and the FA Cup, beginning a period of success for United that would continue for the next two decades.

United was his last club. Cantona retired at the young age of 31. He went on to have a successful career as an actor in theatre and in films. The ultimate rebel had found another way to channel his emotions.

The GOAL
Brazil, 1989
CHEAT!
CHILE STAR IN WORLD CUP SHAME

One of the most dramatic and scandalous moments in World Cup history came when Chile goalkeeper Roberto Rojas was caught cheating on camera. His audacious attempt to stop rivals Brazil from qualifying in the 1990 World Cup led to Chile being temporarily banned from the competition.

Before the 1990 World Cup, Rojas had an incredible career as a goalkeeper. With his thick black hair, straight nose and habit of flying through the air to stop shots, his nickname was El Condor, the condor, after one of the world's largest flying birds. Rojas had played for and captained his country. In 1989, he had just one dream left: to play in a World Cup. Chile had a chance: a two-match play-off against Brazil. The winner would make it to the 1990 World Cup.

Brazil had never missed a World Cup in their history and had never even lost a qualifying match. The first match was in Chile's capital city Santiago. Rojas, the captain, made an important decision before the game had even started. He led his team out of the tunnel before Brazil was ready, so the visitors came out alone, facing a wall of noise and jeers. It set the tone for an aggressive atmosphere. Two players were sent off early.

The game finished 1–1 when Chile equalized through a controversial free kick, quickly taken while their opponents were arguing with the referee. The Brazilians were pelted with batteries and stones as they walked off the pitch. The home fans' behaviour led FIFA to ban Chile from hosting its next match at home. Chile claimed there was a FIFA conspiracy against them. After the game, Rojas was asked why he had brought the team out early. "Against Brazil," he said, "you have to do everything you can to win."

The return match in Rio de Janeiro was two weeks later. Could Rojas inspire his team to a historic victory? It looked possible: he made four fantastic saves and at half-time it was 0–0. But then Careca scored for Brazil to make the score 1–0.

With twenty minutes left and Chile attacking, Rojas suddenly fell to the ground. Someone behind the goal, among the Brazil fans, had thrown a flare onto the pitch which had seemingly hit Rojas. On the ground Rojas appeared hurt. When the smoke cleared, there was blood all over his face. He was carried off. Chile were furious. Their coaches argued with the referee and the Chile players walked off the pitch. They wanted the game abandoned and Brazil eliminated due to the behaviour of their fans.

There was one problem: no one had actually seen the flare hit Rojas. Everyone had seen the flare on the pitch, the smoke around the goal, Rojas on the ground and then covered in blood. But did that mean he had been hit? And if he had been hit, given that a flare is hot rather than sharp, why was he cut and not burned? People suspected that Rojas might be cheating, but without proof things looked bad for Brazil.

These were the days before mobile phones, and TV cameras had no footage: they were following the action at the other end of the pitch. Only one newspaper photographer, Ricardo Alfieri, had his camera trained on Rojas at the moment the flare was thrown. He took five shots of the incident. Cameras back then were different to today. There was no digital processing, or immediate images fed back to a newsroom. Instead, Alfieri had to take his camera-film to a lab to develop the images. The process took four hours. Only then could the world find out what had really happened.

The pictures revealed the true story: the flare, which had been thrown by an excited Brazil fan, had landed behind Rojas. Rojas then took a step back and rolled into the smoke. In the next image, he is covered in blood. What we don't see is what happened while he was in the smoke. But one thing was apparent: the flare did not hit him. How could it have damaged his face, if it landed behind him?

So what had happened? Rojas had hidden a razor blade in his football sock, and in the smoke cut himself on the face. He was so desperate to win, he thought that Chile could make it if Brazil were disqualified. FIFA punished him for his cheating: he was banned from playing football for life and Chile banned from the next two World Cups. The Condor had crashed down to earth.

## EPIC FACTS

- Condors are the largest flying birds in the world with a maximum wingspan of over 3 metres.
- Condors are part of the vulture family and feed off carrion, which are the carcasses of dead animals. They can travel up to 120 miles a day looking for food.
- Condors are not great flyers and often need a gust of wind to get them going!

# THE FOOTBALL TIMES

SPECIAL EDITION — Bournemouth, 2009

## Howe saves Cherries from oblivion in late, great escape

### Dramatic winner keeps Bournemouth up

**Above: Fans hail Howe after memorable victory.**

Eddie Howe was at a New Year's Eve party when he received what he thought was a prank phone call. It was the last day of 2008 and Howe had been asked if he wanted to become coach of his beloved hometown club, Bournemouth. Howe was only 31 and if he took the job, he would be the youngest coach of all 92 clubs in the football league.

The phone call wasn't a prank and the offer was real. Howe had impressed as Bournemouth's youth team coach after injury had cut short his playing career. So when the club sacked its head coach on New Year's Eve, they turned to him.

Howe had a quick think. Bournemouth were ten points adrift at the bottom of the fourth division. The Cherries had started the season with a 17-point penalty because they had run out of money. They could not afford to pay their own players. Relegation would probably kill off the club once and for all. So what did Howe say? Yes!

After all, what else could he say? Howe had supported Bournemouth as a child, joined the youth team aged eleven, and played over 200 times as a centre-back. He was never going to turn them down!

It was his first job as coach and he made an immediate impact. Despite the points penalty, Bournemouth crawled up the table and still had a chance of survival on the final day of the season. Beat Grimsby Town, and they would stay up. Lose, and the club would be relegated, and with no more money, might cease to exist. At half-time, the team was 1–0 down. Howe told his players to stay calm and remember what their individual roles were. Despite the high stakes, his composure seeped through to his players.

Bournemouth equalized early in the second half and just before the end of the game, striker Steve Fletcher scored a dramatic winner. It was the goal that kept the club alive. When the final whistle blew, fans spilled onto the pitch to thank the players. Bournemouth would go on to name a stand after Fletcher. Fans called the match the Great Escape. The greatest moment in Bournemouth history was even made into a movie called *Minus 17*.

But Howe wasn't finished. Due to its financial problems, the club was banned from making any transfers the following season, but still managed to win promotion into the third tier. Six months later, Howe took a job at another club, Burnley, who tempted him as they were in a higher division and didn't have any financial issues. He did not stay long: less than two years later, he returned to Bournemouth to be closer to his family after his mother died. Howe was back in charge of the club of his dreams, and guess what? Bournemouth were on the rise again.

His first season back ended in another promotion, this time to the Championship, the second tier. The next target was the Premier League, but fans never really believed that their club, with its tiny stadium, small budget and dramatic history could make it to the most popular league in the world. Howe had other ideas. In their first Championship season, Bournemouth finished in the top ten. It was a sign of things to come: the following season, they were champions! Howe had led them from the brink of extinction to the top flight – they had made it to the Premier League!

Howe believes the skills that inspired Bournemouth to their Great Escape – hard work, strength of character and the ability to bounce back from disappointments – helped them in the years that followed. Those traits sustained them in the top flight for five years. Bournemouth, with a stadium smaller than some non-league teams, beat the likes of Manchester United, Chelsea, Arsenal and Tottenham Hotspur.

The club's glorious run ended when they were relegated in 2020. Howe, once described as the best young English coach in the Premier League, could not pull off another great escape. The Cherries were pipped at the post. But it was only thanks to Howe that they were still around to play at all.

Home - BOTN News

backofthenet.co.uk/beautifulgame

News | Fixtures | Teams | Tables

# Beautiful game

France

2019

## Artist sells painting of footballers for £17 million

Football can be inspirational in so many ways and sometimes far beyond the world of sport. This story is about how a single match changed the life of the French artist Nicolas de Staël. The creativity and magic he saw on the pitch fired him up with enthusiasm like nothing else had done before.

One day in 1952, de Staël went to watch France play Sweden at the Parc des Princes in Paris. It was an evening game, played under floodlights. The match itself was not particularly memorable, but the whole experience made a huge impact on him.

The bright green grass, the blues and reds of the kits, the dark and menacing sky and the movement of the players all caught de Staël's imagination. He left the stadium buzzing with excitement.

That night he didn't go to bed. He went straight to his studio, and began to paint a picture of the game. He started splashing colour all over a canvas. But it wasn't a detailed picture like a photograph. De Staël's painting looked like a mosaic of different colours: the players were rectangular blocks of colour made from thick brushstrokes.

When he finished the first painting he started another and then another. "I've put the whole French and Swedish teams to work," he said. "What joy! What joy!"

Over the next few weeks, de Staël painted twenty-four paintings inspired by that football match. They are considered his greatest works and their bold, blocky, abstract style brought him international acclaim.

When one of his paintings of footballers was exhibited in New York, the critics loved it. De Staël was talked about in the same breath as other great artists of his era, such as Jackson Pollock (who used to pour and splash paint all over his canvas so it looked like a big colourful mess). An American art dealer paid de Staël a generous salary to paint more and he earned enough to buy a villa in the south of France.

## FAMOUS FOOTBALL PAINTINGS

Artist: **LS Lowry** (English)
Lowry, a Manchester City fan, painted urban landscapes, often depicting local crowds heading to a match. His 1949 work, *The Football Match*, was bought for €5.6 million in 2011.

Artist: **Andy Warhol** (American)
Warhol explored the relationship between art and celebrity. His 1978 work, *Complete Athlete Series*, featured Pelé and was bought for €4.6 million in 2011.

De Staël's football paintings are still considered some of the most interesting and beautiful works of the mid-twentieth century. In October 2019, one of the set, called *Le Parc des Princes*, was sold at auction in Paris for around £17 million, making it the most expensive football painting in history. That's more than most footballers cost!

From watching a lousy match that hardly anyone remembers, de Staël created a masterpiece that has stood the test of time. His experience is also a lesson for us all: the next time you go to a football stadium don't forget your paintbrushes. You could find yourself a new career!

Home - BOTN News ✕

backofthenet.co.uk/twozeronine

News | Fixtures | Teams | Tables

Bhutan

2015

# Time to shine for Two Zero Nine

## World's worst team make history

Every national team dreams of World Cup glory, even the weakest teams representing the smallest countries. Before the 2018 World Cup, the team at the bottom of the FIFA world rankings, at number 209, was Bhutan. They were determined to show the world they were better than that!

Bhutan is a small, mountainous kingdom, on the edge of the Himalayas, in South Asia. Its neighbours are China and India. Its people are proud; so proud, in fact, that they did not like being ranked 209 at all, even though Bhutan had only ever won three matches in the country's history.

Bhutan were drawn against Sri Lanka in the 2018 World Cup preliminary round in 2015. The teams had to face each other home and away, with the overall winner given a place in the Asian qualification group stage. To eliminate Sri Lanka, 35 places above them in the rankings, would be Bhutan's greatest ever footballing achievement. The odds were against them, but they dared to dream!

Bhutan's coach, Chokey Nima, trained the players fiercely for one month just for these two games. Training was so tough that some players vomited. But he was determined to prove to FIFA that their ranking was wrong: "We are Two Zero Nine. But that doesn't mean we are the worst country playing football."

The first game was in Sri Lanka. The Sri Lankan media called Bhutan the "Basement Boys" due to their low ranking and predicted a big home win. The score was 0–0 with just a few minutes left to play, when Bhutan midfielder Tshering Dorji burst into the area and scored an unlikely winner. Bhutan won 1–0! The football federation celebrated by buying every player a bucket of Kentucky Fried Chicken. "Too much chicken," was the team manager's verdict.

The players returned home to a heroes' welcome at the airport. Banners declared: "We Love Team Bhutan" and "Proud of You, Heroes of Druk". *Druk* means dragon in Bhutanese, and the team nickname is the Dragons.

The return match was five days later. Bhutan prepared slightly differently this time. They combined occasional training sessions with many religious visits, travelling deep into the mountains to pray at Buddhist monasteries. On the night before the game, the team drove into the mountains and drank water from a holy fountain in the rock. It was said to bring good luck.

On match day, the team visited another monastery. They sipped holy water again and the captain, Karma Shedrup Tshering, was asked to throw dice. The throwing of dice to make important decisions, known as dice divination, is popular in Bhutan. He threw three threes, making nine. Odd numbers are said to bring good luck. "It was a good throw," he said.

The government gave the whole country the afternoon off to watch the match. Around 30,000 fans cheered when Chencho Gyeltshen, nicknamed the "Bhutanese Ronaldo", put Bhutan ahead after just five minutes. But Sri Lanka equalized just before half-time, meaning the aggregate score was 2–1. If Sri Lanka scored one more, they would progress to the next round, because when the score is tied, the winner is the team that scores more away goals.

The second half got under way. Chencho hit the post. He had a goal disallowed. Sri Lanka then hit the post. There were only minutes left. Whoever scored next would go through. Tension was in the air. And then: a player ran clear. He broke the offside trap and scored! It was … Chencho! The crowd went wild. And so did Chencho: he jumped over an advertising hoarding to celebrate, slipped and hurt himself – luckily not too badly. The final whistle blew. Bhutan had done it!

The Bhutan players were in tears as the enormity of their achievement sank in. Team Two Zero Nine had won two matches in a week and achieved their goal of making it to the World Cup group stage. Their ranking had risen to 177. The players would earn extra money to support their families. The team were going to face future tests against China and Qatar, but in that moment, as the players celebrated in front of the fans, captain Tshering declared: "We let them hear the roar of the dragon."

FOOTBALL
MAGAZINE
France, 2019
UNSTOPPABLE ANT
The Brazilian who played in seven World Cups

Brazilian midfielder Formiga played in her first World Cup in 1995. She has not stopped since. In 2019, Formiga made history when she played in her seventh consecutive World Cup. Seven up!

Formiga grew up with three brothers and her mother in north-eastern Brazil. She started playing football in the street with local friends when she was seven. Her brothers did not want her to play, but Formiga loved football and told them that nothing would stop her. She was right. She moved to São Paulo as a teenager, after a scout spotted her talent. She was called up to Brazil's World Cup squad in 1995, when she was just seventeen and the youngest player on the team.

Formiga's real name is Miraildes Maciel Mota, but now only her family calls her Mira. Everyone else uses her nickname, Formiga, which means Ant. That's because of how she plays: in midfield she is hard-working, tenacious and unselfish – just like an ant! She covers every blade of grass, closes down her opponents and takes set-pieces. She always thinks of other players and sees herself as part of a team whose whole is greater than its individual parts. To start with, she didn't like her nickname. But it stuck with her and now she loves it. "It turned out to be a perfect nickname because it's so consistent with the way I play," she says. "It suits me."

Formiga has won plenty of individual awards for her longevity in the game, and has won trophies in Brazil (playing for São Paulo) and France (for Paris Saint-Germain).

But she was never able to win the World Cup. She came close in 1999, when Brazil finished third, and one step closer in 2007, losing in the final to Germany.

Formiga says the secret of her long career is her dedication. She looks after herself every day, ensuring she properly recovers after every match. Her post-match routine always includes stretching, ice baths, and special exercises devised by her trainer. "Athletes have to take care of themselves, especially if they have a dream they want to fulfil. You have to focus on that and ignore all the distractions and obstacles along the way."

### EPIC FACTS

- Ants are the longest living insects: the queen ant of one species can live for 30 years.
- Ants are one of the strongest creatures: a single ant can carry 50 times its own body weight.
- Ants don't have ears: they listen by feeling vibrations from the ground through their feet.

She did retire before the 2019 World Cup, but was persuaded to come back and help the team as Brazil has not yet produced a player ready to replace her. This is another reason for her long career: there is not enough talent coming through! When she finally does retire, Formiga plans to coach in Brazil and help train the next generation of players.

EPIC STAT

**41 years, 112 days**

The age of Formiga at the 2019 World Cup, making her the oldest player to play in the tournament.

She is already campaigning for better playing conditions, and uses her influence to ask for money, resources and attention to help female Brazilian players. "I know I alone cannot change the sport," she says, "but if I can help the team, that's what I want to do." This ant always puts the team first!

Home - BOTN News

backofthenet.co.uk/viralsensation

News | Fixtures | Teams | Tables

# Viral sensation

Spain

2020

## Romero goes from scoring goals to saving lives

Ana Romero is a Spanish international midfielder whose career has taken her to Barcelona, Ajax and Valencia. She has won four league titles. But she made her biggest impact away from the pitch. In 2020, Romero was playing for Real Betis in her hometown of Seville when the coronavirus pandemic stopped all football.

Romero has a university degree in medicine and, with the permission of her club, applied to work as an emergency doctor in ambulances and hospitals to help patients suffering from the illness. Romero, wearing a mask, gloves and protective clothing, worked night shifts to help any patients with the virus.

Romero was praised by her team-mates and the club itself, who announced: "Ana is great on the field, but even greater off it."

**EPIC FACT**

Another Spanish player, Diego Cervero, followed Romero's example and worked as a doctor during the pandemic. Cervero is a former Real Oviedo striker with over 240 goals to his name. He spent seven years studying for a medical degree and could not wait to help patients in need. "Medicine is a vocation," he said. "I felt I had to help."

Romero felt she had no choice but to step up and use her medical knowledge to help her local community. "If this crisis can teach us anything, it is that we learn what our priorities are, and what really matters. And right now, football is not important."

Romero herself also reminds us what true heroism is: having an impact by thinking of other people, helping your local community and making a difference. This Spanish star is an epic hero!

The GOAL
Sunderland, 2009
PROGRAMME
BEACHED
BEACH BALL WINS THE GAME

Callum Campbell was just like any other sixteen-year-old fan. He supported his team, Liverpool, with a passion. He lived close to Anfield, their home stadium and also travelled to support the team for away matches. In fact, like many supporters, he would do anything for his team. But when he contributed to one of the most surprising goals in Premier League history, it wasn't quite what he might have had in mind.

It was October 2009 and Campbell was nervous about Liverpool's game at Sunderland. It was not only because the Reds were having their worst start to the season for 22 years, but because he was superstitious and had left his lucky beads back at home. It turned out to be a day when his luck had definitely deserted him!

Before the game began, the Liverpool fans behind the goal were singing all the usual songs. As "You'll Never Walk Alone" rang out, the fans played keepy-uppy with their hands, using a Liverpool inflatable beach ball that someone had brought with them. The ball headed towards Campbell, who grabbed it and threw it onto the pitch. By the time the match kicked off, the wind had carried the beach ball into the back of one of the goals. It was the goal Liverpool would be defending in the first half.

A few minutes into the game, Sunderland started an attack down their right wing. The winger jinked into the area and crossed the ball. It was touched back to Sunderland striker, Darren Bent. He was about fourteen yards from goal, just on the left-hand side of the area. He pulled back his foot and fired a shot that was heading straight at Liverpool goalkeeper, Pepe Reina. It would have been easily saved … except for one thing.

In the space between Bent and Reina were two obstacles. One was a Liverpool defender, whose legs were wide apart and his arms tucked into his body. Next to him was the beach ball that Campbell had thrown onto the pitch. During the game, it had rolled out of the goal and back onto the pitch.

Bent's shot went towards Reina. Then it hit the beach ball. The beach ball rolled towards Reina, while the football careered off at the opposite angle towards the goalkeeper's far corner. Reina's first step had been to follow the movement of the beach ball. By the time he realized that the football was heading in the other direction, it was too late. The football had struck the stray beach ball and crossed the goal-line. The ball was in the back of the net and Bent ran off in celebration. Sunderland had taken the lead! Or had they?

This freak event had never happened in a professional match before. Referee Mike Jones was unsure about what to do. He ran over to his assistant and had a quick chat. The pair decided to award the goal to Sunderland, who held on to win the game 1–0. That moment defined the whole match.

After the game, Sunderland manager, Steve Bruce, and Liverpool manager, Rafa Benitez, had no complaints.

But it turned out that Jones had made a mistake. A big mistake! The official laws of football say that if an "outside agent", which is someone or something that shouldn't be there, is on the pitch, the game should be stopped until it is removed. The beach ball was an outside agent, affecting the game, and Jones should have disallowed the goal.

Campbell was horrified when he saw the goal go in. Not only had Liverpool gone behind, but he had contributed to their downfall by throwing the beach ball onto the pitch in the first place! Jones was relegated from Premier League duties the following week, but soon returned to the top-flight. The record books still state that Bent scored the goal. And the beach ball? It now lives in the National Football Museum. We don't think Campbell, the fan who accidentally contributed to Premier League history, will be visiting anytime soon!

**The GOAL**

**Reading, 2006**

# HORROR SHOW!

## THE KEEPER WHO ALMOST DIED

Petr Čech, the former Chelsea goalkeeper, still has the hundreds of cards, letters and get-well messages that he received from fans and fellow players after the injury that left him close to death. They serve as a reminder of what he has been through, what he has overcome – and just how precious life really is.

Čech's life hung in the balance fifteen seconds into a Premier League match against newly promoted Reading in October 2006. Reading winger, Stephen Hunt, in his first appearance and desperate to make a good impression, ran onto a through-ball to edge it past Čech. Instead, his knee accidentally connected with Čech's head at high speed.

The impact was so hard that it fractured Čech's skull, pushing pieces of bone towards his brain. Reports later said that the power of the collision was similar to being in a car crash. But at the time, no one knew this. Čech was dazed but conscious, able to lift his arm and tell the Chelsea doctor that he couldn't see well. He crawled off the pitch, but his condition quickly worsened. By the time an ambulance arrived to take him to a nearby hospital, Čech had fallen unconscious. The game continued. Chelsea won 1–0. Hunt was named man of the match.

Čech, meanwhile, was transferred to the specialist brain unit at a hospital in Oxford, where he underwent emergency surgery to save his life. Surgeons lifted two loose pieces of bone away from the brain and inserted two metal plates above his left ear. The bones could have cut into his brain or damaged blood vessels, both of which could have ended his life.

When he woke from his operation, Čech could not remember anything about the accident. The period from going out to start the match and four days after the operation, when his Chelsea team-mates visited him, is a total blank. He struggled to remember words, and had constant headaches. He couldn't play again for the rest of the season, but was determined to prove the doctors wrong and get back on the pitch.

It turned out that Čech had been born with a thinner-than-average skull because he was one of triplets. This made him more at risk from a head injury. To be able to play safely, specialist equipment manufacturers took 3D scans of Čech's head and made him a protective helmet with shock-absorbing foam on the sides. The helmet protected the metal plates in his skull, while allowing him to hear his team-mates perfectly.

Less than four months after his near-death experience, Čech was back in goal for Chelsea. Unbelievably, he played just the same as before. He displayed the same courage and was not afraid to claim loose balls when opponents were rushing in on him. "When you play in goal, you expect to get kicked," he said. "When the ball is there to be won, I don't consider what might happen."

Čech wore the helmet in every match for the remaining twelve years of his career. He became a Chelsea legend, helping them win four Premier League titles, four FA Cups and the 2012 Champions League final, a match in which he saved three penalties as Chelsea beat Bayern Munich after a dramatic penalty shoot-out.

EPIC STAT

**202**

The record-breaking number of clean sheets kept by Petr Čech in the Premier League. That means he played in over 200 games without conceding a goal!

One of the first things he did after he retired was play in goal for his local ice-hockey team, as that was the sport he grew up loving to play in the Czech Republic. In his first match, he saved a penalty in the shoot-out!

Since Čech's accident, the Premier League has changed its rules around head injuries. Doctors no longer have to wait for the referee to allow them onto the pitch to treat a player with a head injury – and every team must have a doctor on the bench who has completed a compulsory medical course in head injuries. Čech almost lost his life, but he is helping other players to save theirs.

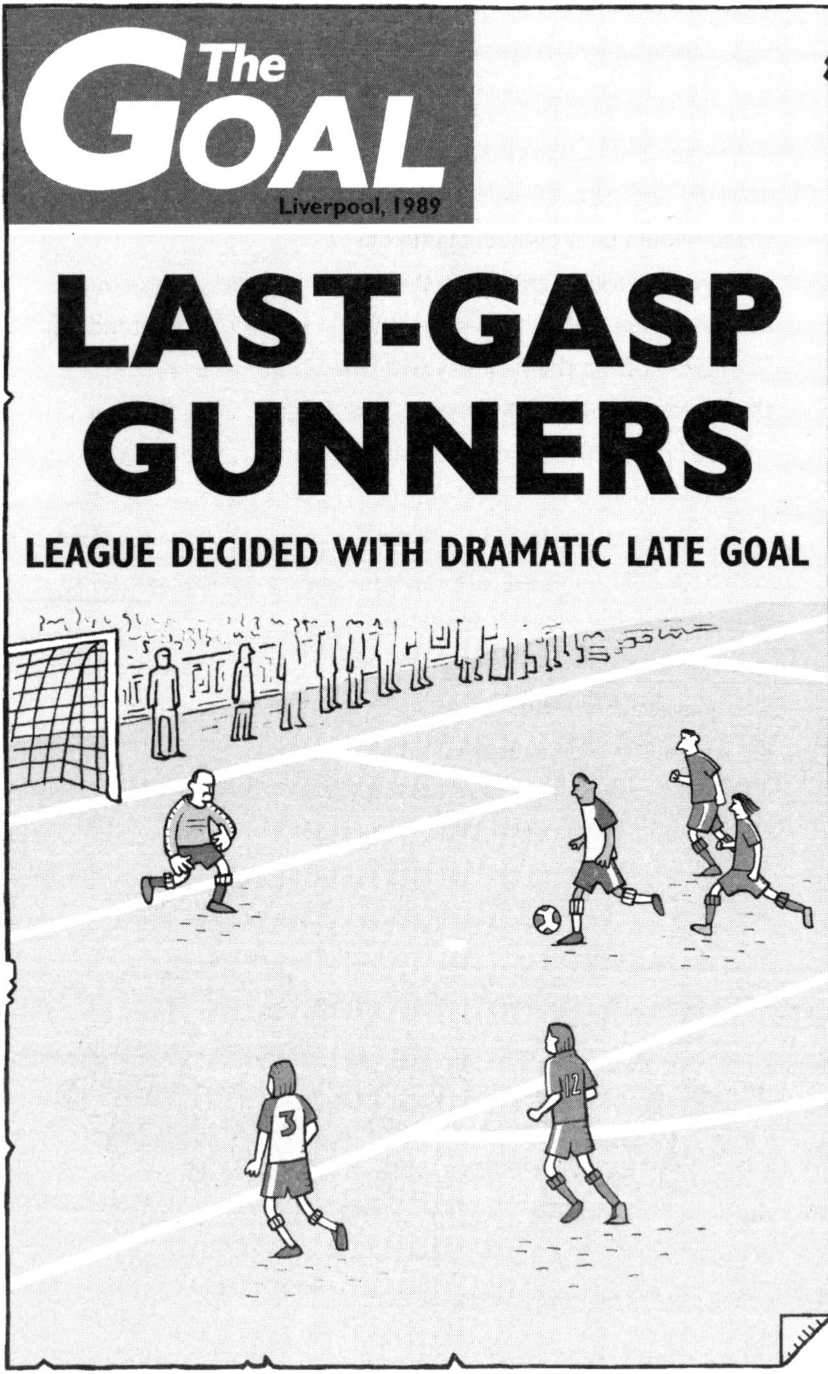
The GOAL
Liverpool, 1989
LAST-GASP GUNNERS
LEAGUE DECIDED WITH DRAMATIC LATE GOAL
3
12

On the last day of the football season in May 1989, Arsenal headed to Liverpool to play in a match to determine the league title. Their task was clear: to win the game by two clear goals, otherwise Liverpool, three points ahead, would be crowned champions.

It was a thrilling ending to the season and the stakes could not have been higher. It was the only time two title contenders have faced off on the final day with the title on the line. Not that anyone expected Arsenal to win. After all, they had not won at Liverpool's Anfield stadium for fourteen years.

A few hours before kick-off, the Gunners manager George Graham was strangely calm. While the players drank tea, and ate toast and honey, he told them he had a plan. He wanted to prevent Liverpool from scoring an early goal, so had picked an extra defender. He told his players not to worry if the score was goalless at half-time. He predicted that Liverpool would get nervous in the second half.

Graham was right. Liverpool didn't score an early goal, although they missed a few chances. And it was goalless at half-time. "Does this feel like a wasted journey?" he serenely asked his players during the break. Early in the second half, Arsenal scored a goal, centre-forward Alan Smith faintly glancing in a free kick. Now Liverpool and their fans were getting nervous.

The clock ticked on: 60 minutes gone, 70 minutes, 80 minutes, 85 minutes, 87 minutes. Arsenal were still leading by a single goal. At this point, one of Arsenal's players fell to the ground with cramp. As he received treatment, a Liverpool player raised one finger and turned to all his team-mates. He urged them to stay focused, shouting, "One minute, just one more minute." He knew that if Liverpool only lost 1–0, they would still be champions.

Liverpool had the ball, but then winger John Barnes lost possession. The ball was passed to the Arsenal goalkeeper, who ignored his coach's shouts to kick the ball as far as he could, instead passing it to a nearby defender. He played it up to Smith, in space, who chipped it over his marker towards midfielder Michael Thomas. The clock had now gone past 90 minutes.

Thomas was outside the area but he lost control of the pass. The Liverpool fans shouted desperately at the referee to blow his full-time whistle. The ball ricocheted off a Liverpool defender. It could have gone anywhere, but it rolled into the area. Still the whistle didn't blow.

Thomas ran towards the ball as the Liverpool goalkeeper Bruce Grobbelaar rushed out. Two defenders closed in on Thomas from behind. "Once I was through, I didn't notice anything going on around me," said Thomas. "It was like time slowed down."

Thomas flicked the ball over Grobbelaar's legs and into the bottom right-hand corner of the net. Somehow, with one of the last kicks of the whole season, Thomas had won the league title for Arsenal. Liverpool's players slumped to the ground in shock. Arsenal were the champions!

This was Arsenal's greatest ever victory. Its impact was even bigger on football. It came when people had fallen out of love with the game, and this was a reminder of its unique drama. The stunning conclusion to the match also helped usher in a new era of football on TV – even if nothing we have seen since has ever been able to match this breathtaking climax!

The GOAL
Indonesia, 2018
NICE ONE SON!
KOREAN STAR WINS GAME TO SAVE CAREER
7

In 2018, South Korea's greatest ever footballer Son Heung-min played the most important game of his life: the final of the Asian Games against Japan.

Win and he would be a national hero.

Lose and he would be forced to leave football for 21 months. His glittering career would be as good as over.

Son's nerve-wracking situation was the result of the law in South Korea that makes military service compulsory for every able-bodied man under 28. Rich or poor, famous or unknown, every South Korean man must spend 21 months in the army before they turn 28.

The only people who are allowed to skip military service are athletes who represent South Korea and win either:

1. The World Cup (tricky as South Korea have never reached the final)

2. Any Olympic medal (Son came close in 2016 but South Korea lost in the quarter-final to Honduras)

3. The Asian Games

Which meant that the last chance for Son, aged 26, to avoid military service was for South Korea to win the 2018 Asian Games final against Japan in Indonesia.

Not only were South Koreans cheering him on but so were fans of his club Tottenham Hotspur, where he was a much-loved and important part of the team.

With so much at stake, the final was tense. Son created excellent chances for his team-mates but they were not able to score. He took a few shots from outside the area, which were saved. After 90 minutes, the score was 0–0.

In extra time, Son dribbled into the penalty area, jinked past his marker and laid the ball back to Lee Seung-woo who drove a shot into the top of the goal. It was 1–0 to South Korea! Minutes later, Son won a free kick, which he curled into the box. There was Hwang Ui-jo to head it home, making it 2–0 to South Korea! Japan managed to pull one goal back but South Korea held on to win 2–1. Son had done it!

He cried tears of joy at the final whistle, hugged his team-mates and threw his coach up into the air in jubilation. The South Korean fans who adore Son were delighted that he was able to skip military service and carry on playing for Tottenham. The Spurs coach was also happy; he picked Son as soon as he returned and partly thanks to Son's goals, the team ended the season playing in the 2019 Champions League final.

Son himself is a fierce patriot and claimed he was just happy to win a trophy. "It was not my aim to avoid military service," he said. "My aim is simply to be great as a footballer." And to prove it, in 2020 he completed the three-week training course given to every South Korean soldier. While he was on his training course, a superb solo goal he scored for Tottenham against Burnley was voted the Premier League's goal of the season. Stand to attention and salute, Son!

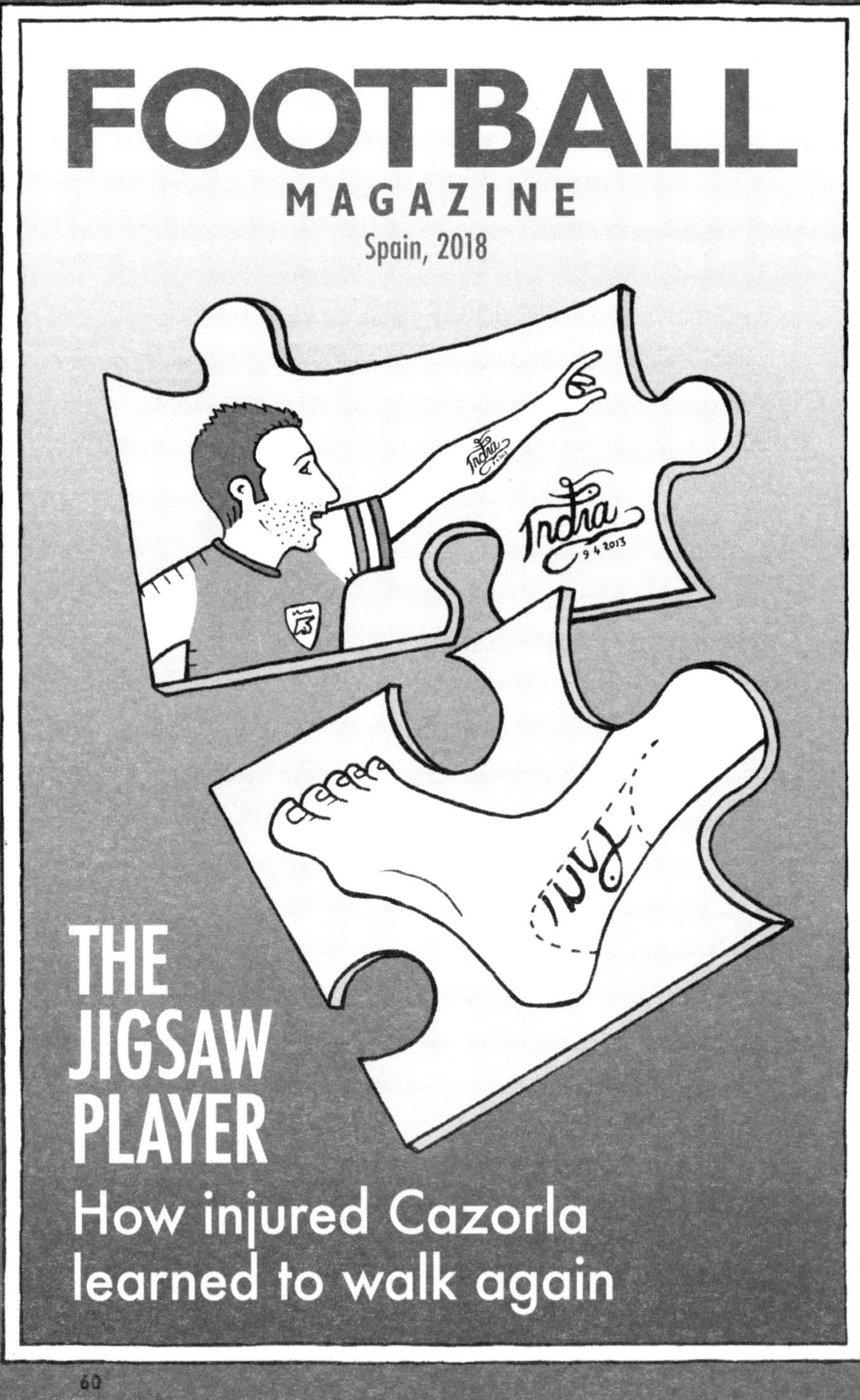
FOOTBALL
MAGAZINE
Spain, 2018
THE
JIGSAW
PLAYER
How injured Cazorla
learned to walk again

Santi Cazorla is a rarity in football: a player who everyone likes, whatever team they support. The midfielder plays with a smile on his face, a glint in his eye and magic in his boots. He helped Spain win two European Championship titles and Arsenal win two FA Cups. And then he faced his biggest challenge of all: to learn to walk again.

In 2013, Cazorla was playing for Spain in a friendly against Chile, when he cracked a small bone in his ankle. He bandaged it up, finished the match and continued playing, even though he was urged to take a break. He played on until another foot injury meant he needed an operation.

He had the operation and was soon out on the pitch again. By 2016, the pain in his ankle had become too much. At the start of every second half Cazorla was in agony, because during half-time, the ankle would get cold and stiffen up. Meanwhile, the wounds from his original foot operation had not healed properly and were leaking pus. It turned out that Cazorla's wound had become infected. Bacteria were eating away at his Achilles tendon, the cord that connects the calf muscle to the heel bone and which is crucial for running.

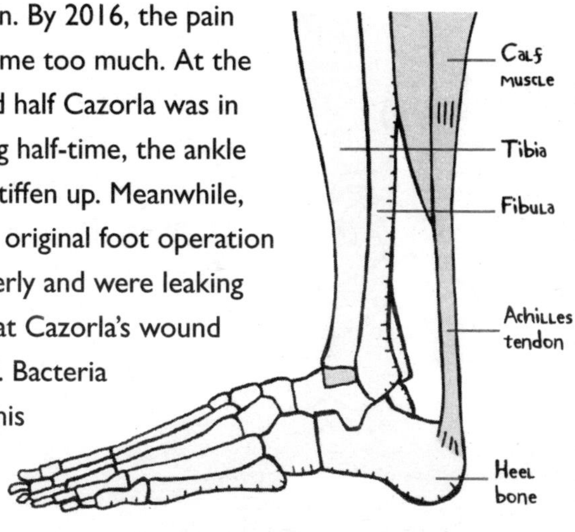


Cazorla went back to his doctor. This time the news was bad. The infection had destroyed around ten centimetres of his Achilles tendon (about two thirds of it) and had eaten into his heel bone as well. The bone was in terrible condition – soft like putty, and with a hole in it.

**EPIC FACT**

The Achilles tendon is named after Achilles, the greatest hero of ancient Greece. His mother Thetis is said to have dipped him in the river Styx to make him invincible: she held him by the heel, which was the only part of him not touched by the water. An arrow wound to his heel killed him. Now the term "Achilles heel" is used as a metaphor, referring to a point of weakness in someone strong.

Cazorla was told that he would never play again. There was a chance that he might lose his leg. The best he could hope for was the occasional walk around his garden. He was devastated, but didn't want to give up. He wanted his two children to see him back on the pitch. In all, Cazorla had eleven operations. Doctors rebuilt the tendon using muscles cut and rolled up from his hamstring, and they inserted a steel plate in his heel to lock it together.

Cazorla describes his body as a jigsaw puzzle because he had so many skin grafts. He has part of his left forearm on his right ankle; some of his thigh on his forearm; part of his leg on his heel; and his hamstring in his tendon. The tattoo of his daughter's name, India, is now in two sections of his body: "Ind" on an arm, where it was originally inked, and "ia" on his ankle.

While he was injured, his Arsenal contract expired and he left the club. In summer 2018, aged 33, he returned to Villarreal, where he began his career. Most people thought his old team were just being nice, offering support to a popular former player whose presence in the dressing room, even if he couldn't play, might just cheer up the team.

That was not what happened. After 668 days out injured, Cazorla played again. In fact, he barely stopped: he played an incredible 46 games for Villarreal that season and scored seven goals, including two against Real Madrid. And for the *ganas*, the desire, that he showed during his tough recovery period, he was applauded at every away ground where he appeared. Thanks in part to Cazorla, Villarreal survived in their fight against relegation.

Cazorla was playing again – and playing well. And so, on an emotional night in June 2019, the player who had been told so many times that his career was over, and that he may not walk again, fulfilled his ultimate ambition. He played again for Spain. He even wore the captain's armband in the second half. Spain won the match, against the Faroe Islands, 4–1. This time, the result didn't really matter. Just by being there, Cazorla had won.

# THE FOOTBALL TIMES

SPECIAL EDITION Liverpool, 2020

## Klopp ends Liverpool's 30-year wait for title

German coach uses defeats to inspire success

**Above: Klopp delighted fans by coaching Liverpool to Premier League victory.**

Jürgen Klopp loves winning because he has lost so often. The German coach made history with Liverpool, winning the Champions League in 2019 and the Premier League in 2020. The league triumph ended a thirty-year drought since Liverpool's last league title.

Throughout his career, he has turned setbacks into positives. As coach for Mainz, a team that had never reached the German first division, Klopp twice came within one match of sealing promotion, only to lose the final games. When Mainz finally went up, in 2004, Klopp said it was his greatest sporting moment.

When coaching Borussia Dortmund, his team finished second in the German league before finally winning it two years running (in 2011 and 2012). At Liverpool, the team lost two finals in 2016, lost the Champions League final in 2018 and came second in the Premier League in 2019, despite losing only one game all season. "Even when you don't want defeats, it is very important to deal with it in the right way," Klopp says. "I would have had plenty of reasons for getting upset and saying 'I don't try any more'. I am a good example that life goes on."

Klopp calls his clear tactical plan – pressing opponents high up the pitch – "heavy metal football". He is also a great communicator and leader: his players trust him and will do anything for him. He also laughs a lot and gives a lot of hugs! "I'm just a normal person," he says.

Liverpool fans have suggested that a statue of Klopp is built outside the club's Anfield stadium. When something similar was suggested at Mainz, Klopp laughed it off, saying statues collect bird poo at the top and dog wee at the bottom. That's Klopp for you: humble and hilarious!

FOOTBALL
MAGAZINE
France, 2019
OUT OF THIS WORLD!
Space fanatic
Lavelle hits the
heights
16

Rose Lavelle hid under the sheets of her bunk bed and cried her eyes out after the USA women's national team lost the 2003 World Cup final. She was eight years old. She made a pledge to herself: that when she grew up she would play for the USA team and stop this happening again. She had no idea how right she would be!

Lavelle was a talented athlete, even if she was always the smallest on every team she played for. She ran faster and jumped further than any of her classmates. She also had an instinctive understanding of space and how it worked in football. When she first played, aged five, most of the players would chase the ball around in a large group. Lavelle would never follow the pack: she would find some space, wait for the ball to emerge, then score.

Even at that early age, she dreamed of playing for USA. It was an English coach who would help make that dream come true. Neil Bradford was her academy coach in her hometown of Cincinnati; he even bought her an England kit that she still keeps in her wardrobe! Bradford encouraged Lavelle to improve her ball skills, first touch, control and vision to avoid stronger players knocking her off the ball. Lavelle spent hours in her backyard perfecting her technique. "He's the reason I fell in love with the game," she said. "He made me who I am today."

Lavelle excelled as an all-action midfielder in every team she played for and was able to turn professional. It was a success she shared with Bradford. But as well as the joy, there was sadness too. Bradford developed cancer and, after a short battle with the disease, he died.

Lavelle was devastated by the death of her mentor and vowed to honour his memory. Her first step was to play for USA, which she did aged 21. Her first match was bittersweet: it was against England, Bradford's home team. USA lost 1–0 but Lavelle was voted player of the match.

Lavelle was confronted with new challenges. Just as she had made her breakthrough, she kept getting injured, and in 2017 she tore her hamstring muscle on three separate occasions. Each time, she took a break and had to work harder to recover her fitness. It was physically gruelling and also mentally tough. There were times when Lavelle wondered if she would ever make the 2019 World Cup.

During this period, she spent ages reading and took inspiration from something she read in a book about astronauts. One former astronaut compared the amount of time spent in space (not much time) to the amount of time spent preparing for it (lots of time). Lavelle realized that football was similar, and that if she wanted to be fit, she had to improve other aspects of her life like her nutrition, recovery and sleep.

At the 2019 World Cup, it seemed that Lavelle had not changed that much from the little kid who hung back from the pack waiting for the ball. She was able to find pockets of space on the pitch, and that technique allowed her to control the game. She was outstanding in the midfield as USA reached the World Cup final.

With twenty minutes of the final left to play, and USA leading 1–0 against the Netherlands, Lavelle dribbled the ball from the centre-circle to the edge of the penalty area. She did a step-over, dropped her shoulder and jinked past her marker before lashing a left-footed shot into the corner of the net. It was a triumph of technique and sealed a famous victory for USA.

Lavelle had played brilliantly. She was voted third-best player in the tournament. She returned to Cincinnati after the World Cup to a hero's welcome. The mayor gave her the keys to the city and declared that July 19, the date of her return home, would forever be Rose Lavelle Day in Cincinnati. Best of all, she had fulfilled that promise she made when lying in a bunk bed all those years ago. Bradford, her first coach, would have been proud.

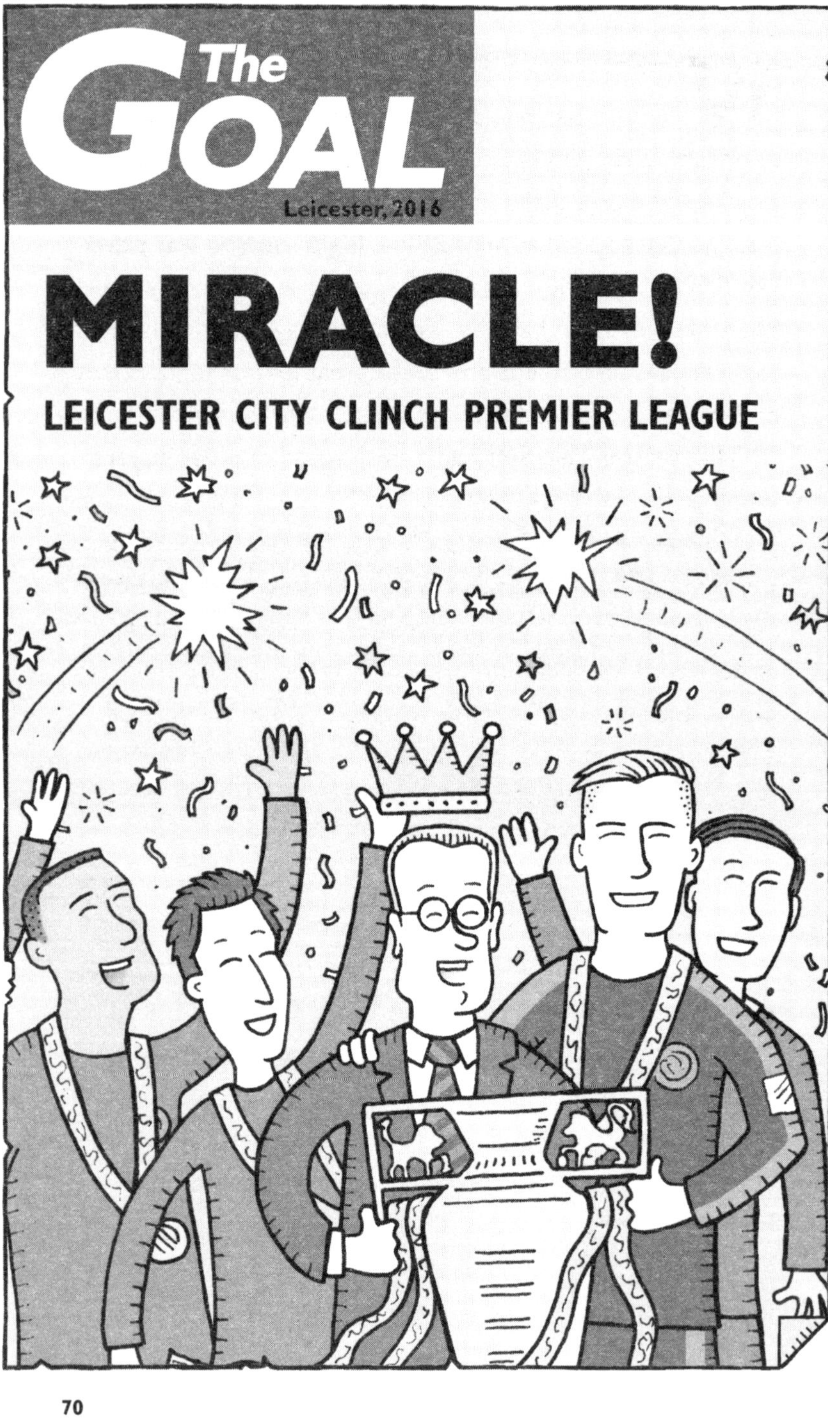
The GOAL
Leicester, 2016
MIRACLE!
LEICESTER CITY CLINCH PREMIER LEAGUE

When Leicester City won the Premier League title in 2016, it was one of the greatest sporting shocks in history. The team had only just avoided relegation the previous year and their chances of winning the league were put at 5,000 to 1. That means if the league season was played out 5,000 times, they would be expected to win it only once! No athlete or team has ever won a sporting event with such slim chances before. But one of the great joys of sport is that sometimes unpredictable things can actually happen…

That season, Leicester had a small squad of older players who had been rejected and released by other clubs, and young players keen to make a mark. Their new coach Claudio Ranieri turned Leicester into a counter-attacking team, who were happy for the opposition to have the ball, but then sprung attacks quickly when they had it. This tactic allowed them to play to the strengths of unknown winger Riyad Mahrez and striker Jamie Vardy, a recent amateur player who early in the season scored in eleven consecutive games, a Premier League record.

At the halfway point of the season, Leicester were top of the table. No one expected them to stay there, even when considering the poor form of the other contenders. Chelsea, Manchester United, Manchester City and Liverpool all had more expensive and better-paid players but were struggling after changes of coach.

Ranieri just told his players to enjoy themselves. He was like a lovable, but eccentric uncle: he rang a bell in training when he wanted to change the drills, shouting his catchphrase: "Dilly-ding, dilly-dong!" He took the players out for pizza after matches in which they kept a clean sheet.

In the space of four days in February, Leicester beat Liverpool 2–0 and Manchester City 3–1. Only Arsenal and Tottenham Hotspur could catch Leicester now. Leicester's next match was against Arsenal, who won thanks to a last-minute goal. Arsenal were only two points behind Leicester in top spot. This was the moment when the Foxes were expected to falter and fall away.

In fact, the opposite happened. Ranieri gave his players a holiday to recover from the defeat and they returned full of energy. They won six of their next seven games. Arsenal won only two of their next seven.

Now it was between Leicester and Spurs. Leicester kept on picking up points and Spurs needed to win at Chelsea to stay in the hunt. The match was played on a Monday night. The Leicester players all went to Vardy's house to watch the game. They were supporting Chelsea. Spurs went 2–0 up before Chelsea scored. Then, with seven minutes left, Chelsea's Eden Hazard curled the ball in from the edge of the area. It was a stunning goal.

The 2–2 result clinched the title for Leicester. Their players celebrated in Vardy's kitchen, cheering, dancing and crying with joy. Fans gathered in the city centre and later toasted some players who joined them to celebrate.

Leicester had confounded the odds and made the most of their luck; their players avoided injuries and the bigger teams had all suffered a slump in form at the same time. Nevertheless, they certainly deserved this victory, unexpected as it was.

On the day Leicester were awarded the trophy, coach Ranieri stood on the pitch with tears in his eyes next to his favourite opera singer, Andrea Bocelli, who had flown over from Italy to sing a famous opera aria, *Nessun Dorma*, in celebration.

Leicester's most famous fan, presenter Gary Lineker, meanwhile, was emotional for another reason; he had made a bet with his fellow presenters on the TV programme *Match of the Day* that if Leicester won the title, he would present the show wearing only his underpants. And that's exactly what he did!

**EPIC FACT**

The star of Leicester's success was N'Golo Kanté, a quiet Frenchman playing in his first season in England. Playing in a two-man central midfield alongside Danny Drinkwater, he was so dominant that people joked Leicester actually had three midfielders: Drinkwater and Kanté on either side of him! Kanté moved to Chelsea and immediately helped them win the Premier League. It was no surprise that when France won the 2018 World Cup Kanté was once again controlling the midfield.

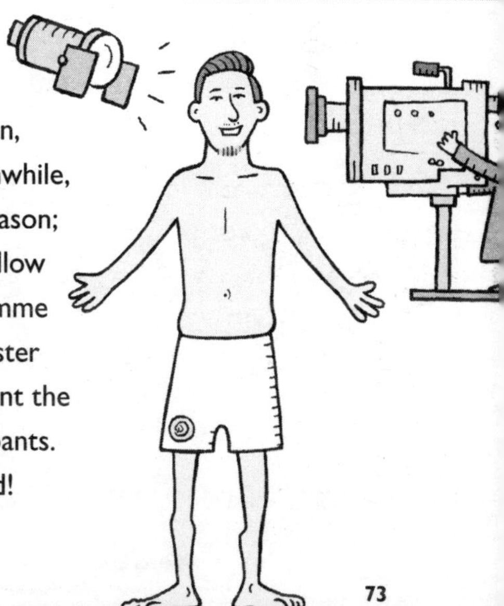

# THE FOOTBALL TIMES

SPECIAL EDITION | Mexico, 1971

## Lionesses are pride of Mexico

### England lose games but win friends at World Cup

**Above: The England women's team suffered three defeats in front of massive crowds.**

The first England women's team to play in a World Cup tournament were left beaten and bruised, but hailed as heroes. A group of young players, some of them still at school, swapped lessons and playing in empty parks for media interviews and a packed stadium with 90,000 boisterous fans banging drums, playing trumpets and singing songs. It was an experience they would never forget.

The year was 1971 and the fourteen players – almost all of them still teenagers – had flown to the tournament in Mexico. For many, it was their first trip abroad. Their previous football experience was playing for local women's teams, where they would be watched by small crowds of family and friends in local parks.

FIFA, football's world governing body, had refused to organize a women's tournament and so another organization, the International Federation of Women's Soccer, set up the Mundialito, a women's World Cup, sponsored by a drinks company called Martini & Rossi. The sponsors paid for everything: travel, accommodation in five-star hotels, kits and a golden trophy. The tournament promised to be worlds away from the England team's usual games.

For nearly fifty years, women's football had been banned by the English Football Association. The FA were worried that the popularity of the women's game would distract people from the men's game and did everything they could to discourage women from playing. That hadn't stopped women from loving football or forming their own teams. It had just made things much harder for the players.

Harry Batt, a bus driver who spoke five languages and coached a women's football team in Luton, decided to ignore warnings from the FA about the England team attending the World Cup in Mexico. He picked the players and organized the trip anyway.

Mexico had hosted the men's 1970 World Cup, so the stadia were tournament-ready and the crowds enthusiastic. When the England team arrived, they were met by the flashes of photographers' cameras and hundreds of cheering fans. They thought someone famous must be on the same flight, until they realized the crowds were there for them! Some of the players were whisked off for a TV interview straightaway, while others were mobbed for autographs.

England's first game was against Argentina. There were over 20,000 fans in the crowd. Argentina were rough on the England team, two of whom suffered bad injuries in the 4–1 defeat. Less than 24 hours later, England faced hosts Mexico in front of 90,000 fans in the Azteca Stadium. Lose and the team would have to go back home.

At half-time England were 1–0 down. The heat, the altitude, the injuries, the fatigue from the recent match against Argentina and the vociferous crowd all helped their opponents. Mexico won the game 4–0. Eight England players ended up in hospital after the match; one had a broken leg, another had a broken foot, three had strained ligaments and others needed extra oxygen.

Yet the manner of England's brave defeats impressed the Mexican fans. The team were asked to stay on to play one more hastily arranged match against France. England's squad were so decimated by injuries, they borrowed three Mexican players. France won 3–2, but England had won the hearts of the host nation.

Back home, it was a different story. The FA was furious that Batt had ignored them by taking an England team to Mexico. They banned his Chiltern Valley team from playing for three months. Many of his players who were briefly superstars in Mexico, mobbed by fans and loved by the media, went back to school as though the tournament had never happened.

It took FIFA another twenty years before establishing a women's World Cup tournament. The FA Women's Super League only turned fully professional in 2018. And yet almost fifty years ago, there was proof that women's football could be as popular as the men's game.

# THE FOOTBALL TIMES

SPECIAL EDITION Portugal, 1967

# Lisbon Lions conquer Europe

## Celtic win European Cup with team of locals

**Above: Celtic celebrate their surprise victory over Inter Milan.**

When Scottish underdogs Celtic beat Inter Milan in the 1967 European Cup final – the forerunner to the Champions League – it was, and remains, one of the most unexpected results in the tournament's history. A true giant-killing!

Ten players in that Celtic team had grown up within ten miles of the Glasgow team stadium, Celtic Park. The eleventh, Bobby Lennox, was born 30 miles away – so still not that far! This band of brothers were friends first, and team-mates second. Growing up they had all shared the same dream: to play in Celtic's famous green-and-white hooped kit.

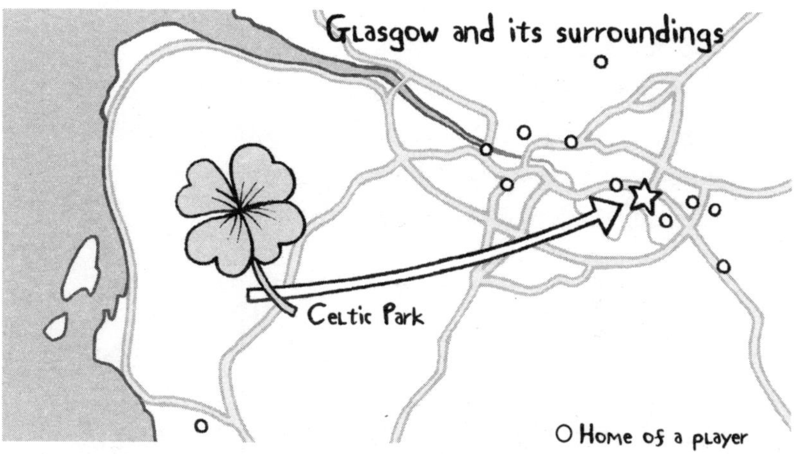


These local boys summed up the ethos of what Celtic was all about. An Irishman, Andrew Kerins, had originally set up the club in 1887. He wanted to give Irish people who had come to live in Glasgow a sense of community through their local football club. The name, the badge featuring a four-leaf clover and even the colour of the kit all reflected Celtic's Irish heritage.

The team of the 1960s was like a family. Each player wanted to show that coming from a small village was no barrier to gaining respect and success. They grew up proud of the team and prouder to represent them. A new coach, Jock Stein, was appointed in 1965 and in his first season, Celtic won their first league title (they would win the next eight in a row). As a result, they qualified for the European Cup for the first time too.

After beating Dukla Prague in the semi-final, Celtic were the first British team ever to reach the final. Awaiting them were Inter Milan, an experienced side who had won two of the last three European Cups. Their coach was Helenio Herrera, famous for inventing *catenaccio*, an ultra-defensive style of football.

The game was played in searing heat in Lisbon. Stein had told his players before the match to even avoid standing near windows because he did not want them to get sunburned. That's how hot it was!

No one gave Celtic a chance, especially after their grizzled opponents took the lead from the penalty spot after six minutes. But Stein had a plan. He had promised fans before the game that the Celtic way was to attack, and even if they lost, they would lose playing that way. And so Celtic kept on attacking. They had so many chances and finally, in the second half, midfielder Tommy Gemmell fired a shot from 25 yards into the top corner. Celtic were level! With seven minutes left, forward Stevie Chalmers escaped his marker and scored.

**EPIC FACT**

Celtic forward Stevie Chalmers was the hero in Lisbon as he scored the winning goal. But it was a miracle Chalmers was even playing! As a younger man, he had contracted meningitis and was given three weeks to live. He received pioneering treatment and was one of the first Scots to survive the illness. Chalmers lived a charmed life!

Celtic held on to win 2–1. Captain Billy 'Caesar' McNeill hoisted aloft the European Cup. Around him, his team-mates rejoiced.

Celtic had bombarded the Inter Milan goal with 39 shots, more than any other team has managed in a European Cup final. Celtic's swashbuckling style made the result a victory of exciting football over boring football. Their supporters, who spilled onto the pitch to celebrate after the final whistle, established the reputation of Scottish fans around the world as passionate and good-natured.

The team of local lads who became kings of Europe were nicknamed the Lisbon Lions. The players kept their friendships going into old age and those who are still alive remain devoted to each other, and the club. Over 50 years later, the result remains the greatest in Celtic's history.

FOOTBALL
MAGAZINE
Liverpool, 2020
KING OF
THROWS
Record-breaker
inspires
Liverpool
to glory

Thomas Grønnemark broke the world record in 2008 for throwing a football further than anyone else. As throw-in coach at Liverpool, he was also the club's secret weapon in the seasons that they won the Champions League and the Premier League. Hands up if you want to know more!

Grønnemark, who is from Denmark, used to be a professional sprinter. He was also in his country's bobsleigh team that almost made it to the Olympic Games. But he was destined to make a bigger splash in the world of football.

A football fan since he was a child, Grønnemark studied the game closely. He knew footballers worked in training to improve their passing, movement, teamwork, corner-routines and penalties. He thought there was another aspect of their game that could be improved: their throw-ins. He was convinced that players were missing a big opportunity.

Grønnemark decided he was going to become football's first throw-in coach. He was always a talented thrower and he picked up knowledge wherever he could: he studied psychology, explored how basketballers create space and used maths equations to calculate angles. He developed exercises on how to keep the ball better from throw-ins.

He thought it would help his new career if he was football's furthest thrower. So in 2008, he tried to break the twenty-year-old world throw-in record of 48 metres, but fell just short. In his attempt the following year, rainy weather made conditions too difficult. After two years and five attempts, in front of a small crowd of 250 fans at a girls' football school, he threw the ball an incredible 51.3 metres. Finally, the world record was his!

Grønnemark's technique was a flip-throw, performing a 360-degree somersault to gain extra momentum so he could launch the ball further. It was also more exciting to watch. "I had training from professional gymnast coaches otherwise it would have been very dangerous!" he told us.

Grønnemark helped one Danish team, FC Midtjylland, win the league title after his training led to them scoring more goals from throw-ins than any other team. In 2018, a German newspaper wrote an article about Grønnemark's work. Liverpool's head coach Jürgen Klopp read it and invited him for a meeting. It went so well that Grønnemark was asked to coach the players the very next day. Liverpool went on to score eight goals from throw-ins that season. "It's about technique but also body language, relations between players, precision, and the mentality of the thrower," Grønnemark explained.

There are around 50 throw-ins per team in every game. That's 50 opportunities to keep or lose the ball. A successful throw-in is one that keeps possession after the throw. The season before Grønnemark started helping Liverpool, their throw-in possession rate was just 45 per cent. That means that after every throw-in, they were more likely to give the ball to the opposition than to keep it. After one season working with Grønnemark, Liverpool's record shot up to 68 per cent. It was the second-highest of all European clubs. The highest, unsurprisingly, was FC Midtjylland.

Liverpool ended their first season with Grønnemark by winning the 2019 Champions League final against Tottenham Hotspur. Their throw-in possession rate reached 83 per cent. In their second season together, Liverpool won the Premier League and scored an impressive fourteen goals from throw-ins. Thanks to this great Dane, let's all throw our hats (and our footballs) in the air!

### HE'S GOT IT LICKED

Grønnemark wanted a sticky material to help his hands grip the ball before his world record throw-in attempt. He went on a children's TV programme in Denmark to test out three different grips: liquorice, prunes, and sweets. He would chew them, then spit on his hands and see which one had the right amount of grip-ability. "They tasted disgusting but it was good fun!" he said. The winner was liquorice; and that's what he used for his successful world record.

THE FOOTBALL TIMES

SPECIAL EDITION France, 2019

# The kiss between rivals

## Harder and Eriksson break the Internet

**Above: Denmark striker Pernille Harder kisses her girlfriend, Sweden defender Magda Eriksson.**

The most famous romantic couple in literature, Romeo and Juliet, came from two feuding families. The most famous romantic couple in women's football, Pernille Harder and Magda Eriksson, come from two feuding football countries: arch-rivals Denmark and Sweden.

**EPIC FACT**

LGBTQ+ stands for lesbian, gay, bisexual, trans, queer and other. It refers to someone's sexual orientation (who they are attracted to) and gender identity (what gender they see themselves as).

Harder is Denmark's most celebrated female footballer, winning European player of the year in 2018. But her Denmark team failed to qualify for the 2019 World Cup as they were beaten in the qualifiers by a Sweden team that included her girlfriend, Eriksson. Awkward!

Harder had no hard feelings and decided to support Eriksson's Sweden for the 2019 World Cup. The Dane even went to the stadium wearing a Sweden shirt to watch Eriksson's Sweden play Canada in a crucial knockout match.

Sweden beat Canada 1–0. As soon as the final whistle blew the Swedish team flocked to their fans to celebrate. Eriksson ran up to Harder and the two women gave each other a heartfelt kiss on the lips. It was a moment that changed their lives.

The picture of the two stars was shared all over the Internet. Both players received hundreds of messages from fans thanking them for their public display of affection after the match. The messages made Harder and Eriksson realize that they were LGBTQ+ role models.

"I don't want to hide anything or be embarrassed about who I love," said Harder. "It's important we are open so boys and girls can see it's OK to love the person you love whether it's a man or a woman."

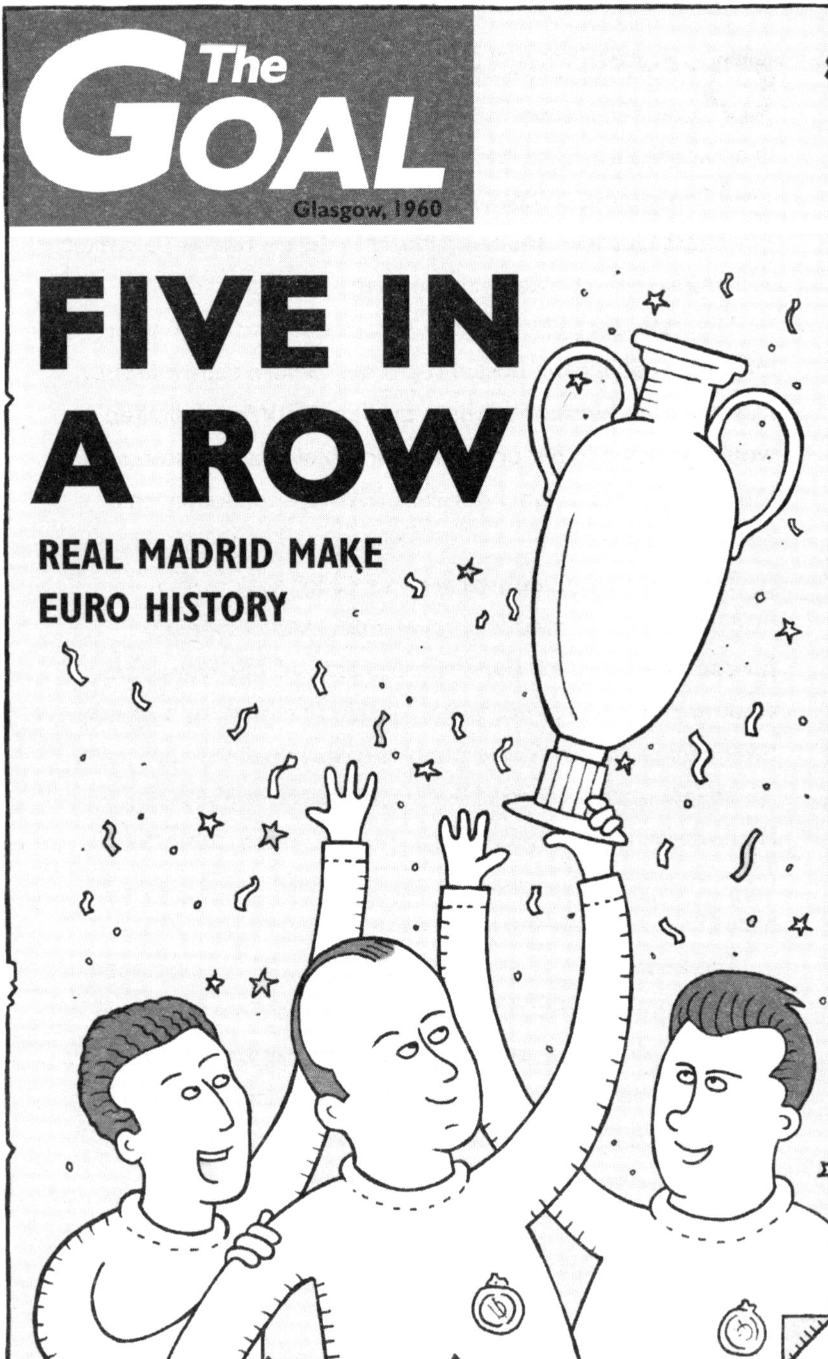
The GOAL
Glasgow, 1960
FIVE IN A ROW
REAL MADRID MAKE EURO HISTORY

One of the greatest games of football ever played, and one of the most significant, began with a surprise goal that shocked a record crowd of over 127,000 fans. It was the 1960 European Cup final, played at Hampden Park in Scotland. The West German side Eintracht Frankfurt – thanks to striker Richard Kress – took an early lead against Real Madrid.

The goal stirred Real Madrid into action and, before too long, they had hit the post three times. Before half-time they had succeeded in scoring three quick goals. What followed would go down in history and secure Real Madrid's status as the most famous team in football. This was the match that created the legend.

The European Cup, a forerunner to the Champions League, had only recently been established to determine Europe's best football team. Sixteen teams from across the continent, all champions of their respective leagues, originally took part in the first edition in 1954. The timing was perfect: shortly after the end of World War II, most of Europe was keen to find ways to come together after years of division. (Not everyone was on board; the English FA did not allow then-champions Chelsea to compete.)

The knockout tournament (there were no group stages back then) was agreed by a committee which included Real Madrid president Santiago Bernabéu. They added one rule that would become important: winning the tournament guaranteed qualification for the next year, regardless of whether the team had finished as champion in their home league.

Real Madrid qualified for the first edition after winning the Spanish league for the first time in twenty years, thanks to a new signing from Argentina called Alfredo Di Stéfano. The striker, who almost joined Barcelona, inspired the team in the first European Cup, helping them beat French side Stade de Reims 4–3 in the 1956 final.

And so Real Madrid qualified for the next tournament as winners (lucky as Athletic Bilbao had won the Spanish league, Madrid finishing third) and again reached the 1957 final. This time they beat Fiorentina, with Di Stéfano once again scoring. The Argentinian made it three in a row with victory over AC Milan in 1958. Reims was on the receiving-end in the 1959 final, as Real Madrid won again.

Di Stéfano had scored in every final and now Real Madrid was on the verge of five successive final wins in a row. Eintracht Frankfurt had beaten Scottish champions Rangers 12–4 over two games in the semi-final. On this memorable Glasgow night, could the Germans possibly get back into the game in the second half?

Madrid began the second half with winger Francisco Gento and forward Ferenc Puskás on the rampage. Puskás had a point to prove: the Hungarian was upset with West Germany for beating his national team in the controversial 1954 World Cup final. (The 1960 final was only able to kick off after Puskás had written a letter of apology to the West German opponents for his comments.) Puskás was unstoppable, scoring two quick goals after the break to seal his hat-trick and make it 5–1.

A bizarre four-minute spell towards the end of the game saw both teams exchange four goals in as many minutes. Puskás bagged one of them and Di Stéfano the other, which was the pick of the night, a mazy run from inside his own half which ended with a virtuoso solo finish. That was his hat-trick goal. The final score: Real Madrid 7 Eintracht Frankfurt 3.

Real Madrid had smashed the record books with this result. They remain the first and only team to win five successive European Cups; Di Stéfano is the only player to score in five straight finals; Puskás the only player to score four goals in one final.

The manner of Real Madrid's performance presented an image abroad of Spain as stylish and successful. The result established Real Madrid as the model of success, glamour and prestige. It is an image that remains to this day.

## HISTORY OF REAL SUCCESS

| Year | Score | Venue | Report |
|---|---|---|---|
| 1956 | Real Madrid 4 Reims (France) 3 | Paris | Recovered from 2-0 and went on to sign Reims forward Raymond Kopa |
| 1957 | Real Madrid 2 Fiorentina (Italy) 0 | Madrid | Almost fell in the first round, needing a replay to get past Rapid Vienna after a 5-5 aggregate draw |
| 1958 | Real Madrid 3 AC Milan (Italy) 2 | Brussels | An extra-time goal from winger Paco Gento edged a tight final |
| 1959 | Real Madrid 2 Reims (France) 0 | Stuttgart | Reims rematch after narrowly beating Atletico Madrid in the semi-final |
| 1960 | Real Madrid 7 Eintracht Frankfurt 3 (Germany) | Glasgow | Beat Barcelona 6-2 in the semi-final before historic final |

Home - BOTN News

backofthenet.co.uk/betterthandiego

News | Fixtures | Teams | Tables

# Better than Diego!

Argentina

2020

## The most talented player no one has heard of

Tomás Carlovich, a midfielder from Argentina, only ever played two games in the Argentinian first division. He never played for Argentina and he never won a trophy. There is hardly any video footage of him in action. Yet he is one of Argentina's most-loved players and the only player Diego Maradona said was better than him. His story shows us that success is not everything in football.

Why was Carlovich, who played in the 1970s, so popular? He hated playing in front of big crowds and he was not interested in fame or money. Football historians believe that he represented what Argentinian people wanted from their football: someone who put talent over trophies and enjoyment over money. His skills were legendary and his mythical story has been passed down for generations. That's why Carlovich is an epic hero!

An elegant midfielder, Carlovich joined first division side Rosário Central when he was fifteen, and made his first appearances for them aged twenty. Before his third game, an away match in Buenos Aires, he jumped off the team bus and went home. That afternoon, he played for a local amateur team instead. He later admitted he never liked being too far from home and he hated playing in front of big crowds. He never played in the first division again.

His coach at Rosário said Carlovich did not have the work ethic and ability to sacrifice his other interests for a career as a professional. After all, Carlovich preferred hunting and fishing to football. And yet, no one ever doubted his ability.

In 1974, Carlovich played in a charity fundraiser against the Argentina national team just before they travelled to play in the World Cup. The plan was to provide an easy opponent for Argentina to win comfortably and gain some confidence. Carlovich had other ideas: his team was 3–0 up at half-time and the Argentina manager is said to have asked for Carlovich to be taken off.

At one point in the game, Carlovich pulled off his signature move: a double-nutmeg. As his opponent Pancho Sá, one of the most successful players of his era, closed him down, Carlovich nutmegged him. Then he turned back and, with his next touch, flicked the ball through Sá's legs the other way as he turned around. Sá couldn't believe it. The crowd went wild. This move secured the legend of Carlovich.

Carlovich spent most of his career playing for Central Córdoba in the second and third division. He was a great footballer but not a great professional footballer. In that respect, he symbolized a romantic type of football that put his own fun and enjoyment before anything else, including his team-mates. He once even got himself sent off so he could catch a bus back home in time for Mother's Day!

In 1976, he was called up to the Argentina national team but he never turned up. He had called the coach and said

he had gone fishing and the river flooded and he couldn't make it. Can you imagine making that excuse if you missed an opportunity like that?

After he retired, Carlovich was asked if he would have done anything differently in his career. With tears in his eyes, he responded: "No, sir, don't ask me that." Did he regret not taking football more seriously when he was younger? Did he wish he had made different choices and worked a bit harder? Perhaps his tears gave him away.

**EPIC FACT**

Carlovich's nickname was El Trinche, which translates as The Fork. In keeping with the mystery surrounding much of his life, no one knows for sure why he was called that. Perhaps his skills were too sharp for defenders, or just very tasty!

In 2020, Carlovich met Maradona, who signed a shirt for him. Maradona wrote: "You were better than me." Carlovich was emotional at the gesture and claimed he could now die in peace. Shortly after, Carlovich was robbed and attacked while riding his bike home. He banged his head and died two days later. Argentina football fans mourned a true talent – and a lost career that could have been so different.

The GOAL
France, 2019
RAPINOE RULES!
MEGAN TOPS TRUMP IN USA ROW
USA
USA

Megan Rapinoe dyed her hair bright pink for the 2019 World Cup in France, but that was only one of the reasons the USA winger stood out. She became its most talked about player because of her goals, and also because of a public row with the most powerful person in the world, Donald Trump, the president of the USA.

Rapinoe was USA captain in 2019, and had been a key part of the team that had won the previous World Cup. She is also a well-known campaigner for equality and tolerance. It was her decision to speak out on these issues that drew the president's fury.

In the USA, when the national football team wins the World Cup, it is traditional to pay a visit to the president at his residence, the White House. But Rapinoe said that if her team won she would refuse to go. She said her refusal was because she disagreed with President Trump's attitude towards women and Black people.

It wasn't the first time that Rapinoe has spoken up for her beliefs, but never before had she done it so prominently at such a crucial time for the team.

When President Trump heard about her comments he was furious. He said she should go and win the tournament before speaking out. And he warned her not to disrespect her own country. Never before has the leader of a country had such a public falling out with the biggest star in its national team.

The row threatened to overshadow the USA's campaign to retain the title they won in 2015. But it also gave Rapinoe a double incentive to win the trophy – to achieve glory for her team, and to settle a score with the president.

The pressure on Rapinoe was enormous going into the quarter-final against hosts France. But it took just five minutes for her to make her mark, with a smart goal from a free kick outside the area.

She ran to the touchline with her team-mates behind her, and faced the cheering crowd with her arms spread wide, and chest out. The goal celebration made her look defiant and proud, and it became known as The Pose. "I'm looking at myself as a performer and trying to entertain," she explained. "It's sort of a funny playful pose."

Rapinoe scored again in the second half; it was the crucial winning goal as France netted a late consolation. USA had reached the semi-final.

Their opponents were England, but Rapinoe was not in the starting line-up. The selection stunned everyone: had she been dropped for her celebration against France? For her row with Trump? Christen Press was Rapinoe's replacement, and she scored in a 2–1 win. What would happen in the final?

It turned out that Rapinoe had a slight hamstring injury and was not fit enough for the semi-final. She was back in the team for the final, though – which was just as well, because Rapinoe was back on the scoresheet. She opened the scoring with a neat penalty in USA's 2–0 win over the Netherlands.

USA were the winners of the 2019 World Cup. Rapinoe scooped the Golden Boot for top goal-scorer. Later that year she also won the Ballon D'Or for the world's best player.

Rapinoe's triumphs in 2019 were especially sweet because she had also silenced her most high-profile critic, President Trump.

And did she – or the team – visit President Trump at the White House? What do you think? Of course not! Megan Rapinoe is a star who sticks fiercely to her principles.

# THE FOOTBALL TIMES

SPECIAL EDITION — Spain, 2009

# The late-night phone call that turned Messi into a genius

## Pep's pep talk changes football history

**Above: Lionel Messi receives a late-night call from Barcelona coach Pep Guardiola.**

Late on the night before Barcelona played a crucial league match against their fierce rivals Real Madrid, Lionel Messi received a phone call from his coach. It was 10 p.m. and the coach, Pep Guardiola, told Messi to come to his office immediately.

Guardiola had spent the previous two days watching videos of Real Madrid matches, and he had finally spotted a weakness. Their meeting that night changed the lives of both men. You could also say that it changed football for ever.

Guardiola showed Messi the video, explaining how Madrid played with three midfielders pushing forward, and two centre-backs staying back. Guardiola paused the video, pointing out the large empty space between their midfield and defence in the pitch's central area. That's where he wanted Messi to play.

It was 2009. Messi was 22, and at that stage had mainly played as a winger. He was to start the game as usual on the wing, and switch to this deeper central position when Guardiola gave him a sign from the touchline.

Only a few minutes before kick-off, Guardiola told Messi's team-mates about the new plan, ordering them to give Messi the ball whenever he was unmarked. Ten minutes into the match, the score was goalless. Guardiola gave Messi the signal, and he moved position. Whenever he had the ball, Madrid did not know what to do. If the defenders pushed up to tackle him, Messi threaded a pass between them for the attacking wingers to run onto; if they stayed back, he dribbled past them at speed. Madrid had no answer to the conundrum. Messi scored two goals and Barcelona won 6–2. His new position, called the false nine, was born.

Madrid were not the only ones who could not find a solution to Messi's new position. Suddenly he had defences bewildered and coaches befuddled. No one could stop him! That season, Barcelona made history by winning every competition they played in, including La Liga, the Champions League and the Club World Cup. No wonder they were the best team in the world: they had the best coach, the best player and now the best tactics!

Messi's change in position kick-started a run of scoring goals that has never been seen before or since. He scored over 100 goals for Barcelona over the next two seasons before breaking all records in 2012, with an incredible 91 goals in 69 matches. His league tally of 50 goals was higher than the tallies of thirteen other sides in the league!

Messi has redefined what we consider possible on the football pitch. His goal numbers suggest he is selfish, but he is not. He sets up almost as many goals as he scores. In the past, anyone who managed 30 goals over one season was seen as exceptional. Messi has topped that number for TWELVE seasons in a row! Any player who wins one Ballon D'Or is a true great. Messi has won it six times.

Messi has consistently made the extraordinary seem ordinary. His performances have left experienced football writers running out of superlative words to describe his accomplishments. This is why, when asked about the greatest footballer ever to play the game, Guardiola says: "Don't write about him, don't try to describe him. Just watch him."

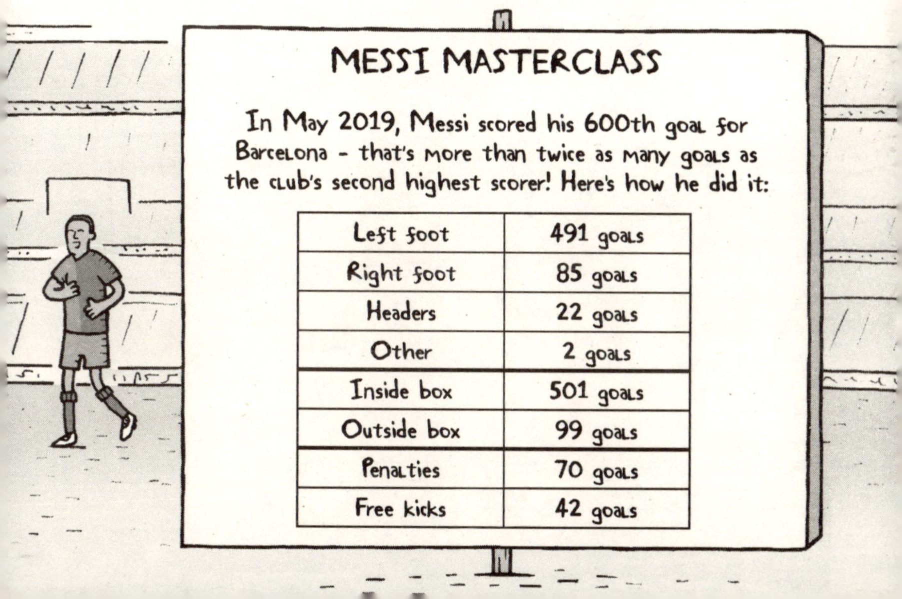

## MESSI MASTERCLASS

In May 2019, Messi scored his 600th goal for Barcelona - that's more than twice as many goals as the club's second highest scorer! Here's how he did it:

| | |
|---|---|
| Left foot | 491 goals |
| Right foot | 85 goals |
| Headers | 22 goals |
| Other | 2 goals |
| Inside box | 501 goals |
| Outside box | 99 goals |
| Penalties | 70 goals |
| Free kicks | 42 goals |

Home - BOTN News

backofthenet.co.uk/sixofthebest

News | Fixtures | Teams | Tables

# Six of the best

London

2019

## Double hat-trick for Dutch star

We know that football is a team sport. But occasionally, an individual delivers a performance so dominant, so impressive and so exciting, that it writes that player into the history books.

Vivianne Miedema is one such player. She grew up in a sporty family in the Netherlands. When she was eighteen months old, she would kick a ball about with her dad on his breaks from working at the family restaurant. Miedema started playing as a striker for Dutch club Heerenveen aged just fourteen, at the same time as studying hard at school. At eighteen, she moved to Germany to play for Bayern Munich, winning the German league twice.

By now she was a Netherlands international, and was one of their most important players when they won the 2017 European Championships. She scored four goals in the tournament, including two in the final against Denmark.

One year later, she joined Arsenal and made an immediate impact. Her twenty-two goals in twenty matches helped the club win the league title. Miedema was the league's top scorer and voted player of the year. In the summer of 2019, she starred on the international stage again: one of her goals at the 2019 World Cup took her to 60 for the Netherlands, and she became their all-time leading scorer. She played in all seven games as the team reached the World Cup final.

Her form continued into the following season at Arsenal. She scored four goals in a Champions League quarter-final win at Sparta Prague, in the Czech Republic, and another three in the home game.

By the time Arsenal hosted Bristol City in December 2019, Miedema was in the form of her life.

It was an important fixture in Arsenal's title challenge. The team was joint top of the table, but behind Manchester City on goal difference. They needed the win. They got off to the perfect start: after four minutes, Miedema fired in a pinpoint cross for Lisa Evans to tap home. Two minutes later, Miedema crossed for Leah Williamson to head in, making it 2–0.

Then Miedema showed what she can do in front of goal: her smart control, quick turn and shot made it 3–0. Her tap-in made it 4–0. Five minutes later, she knocked in Evans's cross for 5–0. Miedema had scored a hat-trick in the space of twenty minutes! But she was not finished yet.

Shortly after half-time, Miedema swept in a curling right-footed shot to make it 6–0. That became 7–0 when captain Jordan Nobbs prodded home her brilliant teasing ball across the six-yard line. Miedema now had four goals and three assists. Enough? Not quite…

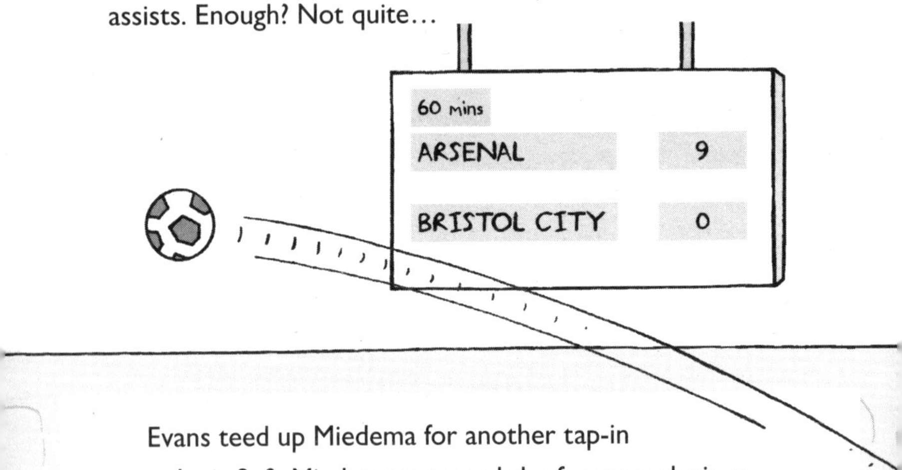


Evans teed up Miedema for another tap-in to make it 8–0. Miedema returned the favour, a glorious chipped pass from outside the area, which Evans volleyed past City's beleaguered goalkeeper for 9–0. The two combined again for Miedema to score her sixth goal. A double hat-trick!

Miedema celebrated the same way as she had for her previous five goals: pointing to the person who gave the assist and walking over to thank her. What a polite team-mate!

After 65 minutes, the score was Arsenal 10 Bristol City 0. Miedema had scored six and set up four. No other player has ever dominated a match quite like it.

Arsenal scored one more and City pulled a goal back with a few minutes left. The final score: Arsenal 11, Bristol City 1. It was a record victory in the women's top division.

When the final whistle blew, the crowd acknowledged Miedema's historic individual performance. "I felt really good today and I was probably happier with my assists," admitted Miedema, who does not like to be the centre of attention. "I just want to be that player who helps the team and I'm happy that we won."

THE FOOTBALL TIMES

SPECIAL EDITION London, 1953

# The magnificent march of the Mighty Magyars

## Puskás inspires Hungary to 6–3 triumph

**Above: Hungary goalkeeper Gyula Grosics celebrates his team's sixth goal.**

Hungary is a small country in Eastern Europe and these days is hardly known for its football. Yet in the middle of the last century, Hungary's national team was the best in the world. That team is remembered, in particular, for two famous matches: an unforgettable friendly against England at Wembley, which changed the course of English football, and the greatest ever reversal in a World Cup final.

In 1953, more than 100,000 fans came to Wembley to watch England play the team known as the Mighty Magyars. (Hungarians refer to themselves as Magyars.) England had never lost a game at Wembley since the stadium was opened in 1923, and the fans were confident the team would win.

The Hungarians, however, were unbeaten since 1950 and were reigning Olympic champions. Their star player was the stocky, barrel-chested Ferenc Puskás, one of the greatest strikers in the history of the game. The match promised to be a classic, and it certainly was!

Within a minute England were a goal down. By twenty-seven minutes they were 4–1 down, with Puskás netting two. The final score was England 3 Hungary 6, which remains England's heaviest ever home defeat.

The match was a huge humiliation for England, exposing the team as out of touch with the latest football innovations. The Magyars played with greater technical skill, fitter players and a more versatile tactical system in which team members changed positions. It also helped that most of the Hungary team played at the same club, Budapest Honvéd, in Hungary, so were more used to playing together than the England team.

A few months later, the teams faced each other for the return match in Budapest, the Hungarian capital. Would England retrieve some pride? Not at all! The Magyars were even more dominant, winning 7–1, which is still England's heaviest defeat of all time. Ouch!

Hungary were on a roll. They entered the 1954 World Cup as favourites. In the group stage they were sensational, beating South Korea 9–0 and West Germany 8–3. In the final, held in the Swiss capital of Berne, Hungary met West Germany again. It was a repeat of the first round match that Hungary had comprehensively won. Surely that meant the title was theirs! Hungary were 2–0 up within six minutes, with their hands almost on the trophy. But then fate intervened. West Germany turned the game around and won 3–2, their first ever World Cup victory.

The result is considered one of the greatest upsets in World Cup history. The dramatic reversal of fortune led to the game being known as the Miracle of Berne. The reasons for Hungary's defeat are still debated to this day. Was it because the pitch was waterlogged, and the Germans used screw-on studs for the first time, giving them an advantage? Was a Puskás goal unfairly marked offside? Berne-ing questions!

Yet even though West Germany were the winners, the Hungarian team entered the history books. Their records of most goals scored in a World Cup (27) and the highest average goals per game (5.4) have never been surpassed.

**EPIC FACT**

The English word "coach" comes from the Hungarian town Kocs, where in the fifteenth century they designed a type of horse-drawn cart with metal suspension. The word later gained a new meaning as someone who trains athletes, since the coach helps to "transport" athletes to their goals.

Hungary changed international football by demonstrating innovative tactics that were soon copied by other teams. But nowhere did Hungary have more effect than on England. The Three Lions' humiliation by the Magyars at Wembley ended England's sense of complacency. England coaches began to look to Europe for new ideas. England soon copied the Hungarian idea of building the national team around a group of players from the same club. When England won the 1966 World Cup, the core – Bobby Moore, Geoff Hurst and Martin Peters – all played at West Ham United.

Hungary has yet to return to the peak of those years, but their golden team of the 1950s is remembered as one of the best that have ever played.

# THE FOOTBALL TIMES

SPECIAL EDITION Oxford, 1994

## Redknapp picks mouthy fan as second-half substitute

### Delivery driver Davies makes West Ham debut

**Above: Fan Steve Davies plays for West Ham in a surprise substitution by coach Harry Redknapp.**

Steve Davies grew up loving West Ham United. When he was a teenager, he went to all of their matches. His mum would cut out tokens from washing powder boxes so he could buy discounted train tickets to cheer them on. He grew up, got married and named his son after his favourite West Ham player, Trevor Brooking.

When he was in his late twenties, Davies had a job as a delivery driver and something unexpected and amazing happened to him. He fulfilled the ambition of every football fan in the world, and proved that even our most improbable dreams can come true.

It was 1994, and Davies had decided to watch West Ham play a pre-season friendly match at Oxford City, with his wife Kelly and another friend, Bazza. They found a spot close to the away team dugout, and before kick-off, had a short conversation with West Ham's assistant coach Harry Redknapp. That brief chat would not be forgotten.

West Ham scored two goals in the first half, but Davies wasn't impressed with Hammers striker Lee Chapman. When he lost yet another battle with his centre-half, Davies shouted at him: "Get up, you're useless!" As half-time approached, Redknapp started planning which subs to bring on. He had heard Davies moaning throughout the first half. He turned to him and said:

Davies thought Redknapp was joking, but Redknapp invited him down the tunnel and into the dressing room. Redknapp told Chapman he was being subbed off and that Davies would replace him. Chapman just nodded. He asked what size boots he wore, and sent the kit-man to get him a kit. Davies received an encouraging slap from captain Alvin Martin, and walked out with the West Ham players in the second half. He couldn't believe what was happening! Davies was now on the pitch playing with his heroes. He thought Redknapp would replace him after a few minutes – having made his point – but he did no such thing.

Davies was a heavy smoker and had drunk two beers during the first half. It was not how anyone else had prepared for the match. His legs were shaking for the first five minutes of the second half, but he stayed on the pitch. With twenty minutes left to play, West Ham's winger Matty Holmes beat his marker and crossed. Davies took a clumsy touch and entered the penalty area. The Oxford goalkeeper came rushing out to narrow the angle. Davies kept his head down and hit it. The ball flew into the bottom corner of the net! Davies ran away in celebration, extending his arms and taking in the congratulations of his team-mates.

He briefly bent his head in disbelief. In the stands, Bazza and Kelly were going crazy. Even Redknapp, who looked up to the sky, couldn't believe it. He had replaced a £1 million striker with a random fan, who had scored! "It was like time had stood still – it was the greatest moment of my life," said Davies.

Davies was exhausted after that. West Ham won the match 4–0 and as quickly as his adventure had begun, it was over. The kit-man demanded his number three shirt back, as it was needed for the following week's Premier League match against Newcastle United. Within 25 minutes, he was back in the car with his friends, fighting traffic to get home.

**EPIC STAT**

**1,395**

Number of professional matches Harry Redknapp watched as a head coach, in a career lasting 34 years and spanning seven different clubs: Bournemouth, West Ham, Portsmouth (twice), Southampton, Tottenham Hotspur, Queens Park Rangers and Birmingham City.

"I wasn't trying to make him look silly," Redknapp later confessed. "I thought I'd make his day. I could see he loved West Ham. He'll never forget it as long as he lives. He came on, ran around, loved it, scored a goal. He played for West Ham!"

One week after selecting a fan to play in a match, and seeing him score, Redknapp was promoted from assistant coach to head coach. He was successful too, leading West Ham into fifth place. Davies also went on to bigger things. He launched his own courier company.

There's a twist in this story and it's one that Davies doesn't enjoy sharing: he was offside. His goal was disallowed. But does it really matter?

FOOTBALL
MAGAZINE
Yugoslavia, 1976
PENALTY GENIUS
Inventor Panenka
shares his secret

Antonín Panenka invented a new type of penalty so brave, risky and skilful that it has been named after him. The penalty was the winning kick for Panenka's country Czechoslovakia in their only major tournament final back in 1976. Now, the "Panenka" – a slow, chipped penalty down the middle of the goal, over the goalkeeper's despairing dive – is revered as the ultimate display of footballing technique.

The distinctive spot-kick only came about because, two years before, Panenka missed two penalties in one game for his Czech team, Bohemians. The midfielder was so upset with himself that he resolved to practise harder. For the next two years, after every training session, Panenka stayed behind to take penalties against Bohemians' goalkeeper, Zdeněk Hruška. They would bet on the outcome of the penalties, usually with chocolate. Panenka lay awake at night thinking of strategies to win more treats. "The more chocolate I won, the bigger I got!" he told us when we flew to meet him near his home in the Czech Republic.

Panenka discovered that if he kicked the ball too hard down the middle, Hruška could save it using his legs. "But if the contact with the ball is lighter, he can't dive back to the centre if he has already picked one side," Panenka said about his realization.

Panenka started practising his penalty in Czech league games. He knew he was onto something when he chipped the ball down the middle against keeper Ivo Viktor, his team-mate for the national team. Viktor knew about his technique but still couldn't stop it! Like many goalkeepers, he felt he had to dive in one direction to show he was trying to save the penalty.

Panenka's moment of glory came in June 1976 in Belgrade, in what was then Yugoslavia. Czechoslovakia had drawn 2–2 in the Euros against West Germany, the reigning world champions and overwhelming favourites to win. This was the first time a penalty shoot-out was used to decide a major tournament. The Germans were unprepared: they had not practised penalties, did not know who was going to take one and only had one regular penalty-taker in their team.

The Czechs were 4–3 ahead when German defender Uli Hoeness kicked his penalty over the crossbar. Panenka stepped up, knowing that if he scored, the victory was secure. Two years of practise were about to be distilled into one kick: all those efforts against Hruška (and all that chocolate!), hours of honing the chip, perfecting the approach, convincing the goalkeeper. Viktor begged Panenka not to try it, but this was his time.

"I saw myself as an entertainer and I saw this penalty as a reflection of my personality," Panenka explained. "I wanted to give the fans something new to see, to create something that would get them talking. To come up with something at a moment when no one expects it. I wanted football to be more than just kicking a ball."

And so it proved. Panenka hit the perfect Panenka and Czechoslovakia became European champions.

The impact of Panenka's penalty went far beyond the Czech success. Germany learned from the defeat and, over the next forty years, won its next six shoot-outs (including two against England). Great players like Zinedine Zidane and Andrea Pirlo scored Panenka penalties in big games. Panenka's moment of genius reminds us that sometimes what you do is not as important as how you do it. Panenka saw himself as an entertainer more than an athlete. If he was going to score that penalty, he was determined to do so in his own style. His penalty is a piece of art whose legacy still entertains us today.

FOOTBALL
MAGAZINE
Sweden, 1958
DREAM TEAM
Pelé and Garrincha create the beautiful game

Brazilians Pelé and Garrincha were one of the greatest partnerships in international football. They were the key players in Brazil's most successful era, in which the country won three World Cups and became known around the world for its exciting, attacking style of play. In the forty games that Pelé and Garrincha played together, Brazil never lost.

Their success together began at the 1958 World Cup in Sweden, although not immediately. Neither player was picked for the first two matches, in which Brazil struggled. Coach Vicente Feola chose them to start the third match, against the USSR, and his decision changed football for ever.

Pelé was seventeen, the youngest player in the tournament. He was unknown on the world stage, but had been a goal machine for his club Santos since his debut aged fifteen. Garrincha, aged twenty-four, was a winger for Botafogo. His trademark dribbles made him almost impossible to mark.

As soon as the match started, Brazil's two new weapons fired themselves like missiles at the opposition. Within 40 seconds, Garrincha hit the post. A few seconds later he passed to Pelé, who also hit the post. After three minutes of relentless pressure, Brazil's other striker, Vavá, scored the opening goal.

With Pelé and Garrincha in the team, Brazil captured the hearts of football fans around the world and they won the 1958 World Cup with a class of football never seen before. The country won a second time in 1962 and a third in 1970.

Pelé and Garrincha were the two geniuses who unleashed the potential of Brazil. When they were on the pitch together, the team were – literally – unbeatable. More than any other players, they established Brazil as the most successful football nation of all time.

Home - BOTN News ×

backofthenet.co.uk/phenomenalphonzie

News | Fixtures | Teams | Tables

# Phenomenal Phonzie

Germany

2019

## Speedy teen's amazing journey to the top

Alphonso Davies ran over half the length of the pitch, outsprinted two markers, and fired in a pinpoint cross for Bayern Munich team-mate Robert Lewandowski to score another goal. It was the final one in Bayern's 3–0 Champions League win at Chelsea, and announced Davies, then only nineteen, as a top player to a global audience. His journey from one end of the pitch to the other, though, was nothing compared to how far Davies, who is called Phonzie by his team-mates, had travelled to get to that point.

Davies was born in a refugee camp in Ghana, a country in west Africa. He parents had fled there from nearby Liberia during that nation's brutal civil war. A refugee camp is a temporary settlement built to accommodate people who have fled their homes for their own safety. Buduburam, where Davies was born, is the biggest camp in Ghana, with a population of 42,000.

Life in the camp was difficult. Every day was a battle to survive as Davies's parents did not have enough money to buy him food or clothes, or to send him to school.

The family applied for resettlement, which is when refugees are allowed to move to a country where they can stay for good. This affords them the same opportunities and rights – for example, education and healthcare – as all citizens. The family moved to Canada in 2006, when Davies was five years old.

In Canada, the family found fresh opportunities. Davies and his two younger siblings went to school, while his parents worked.

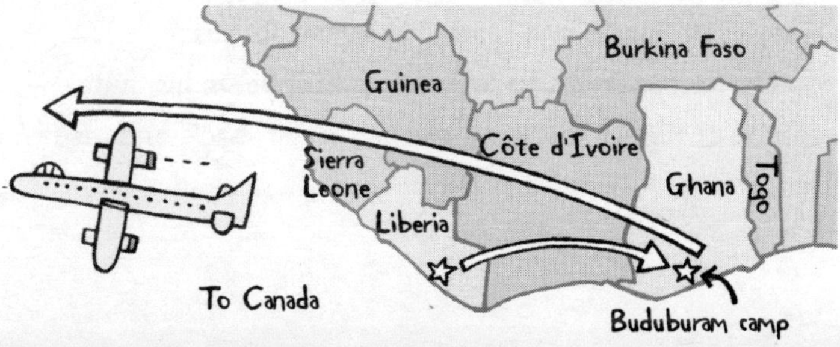

He started playing football in an after-school programme designed to give children the chance to play sport. Davies loved the game because he was with his friends. He didn't know how good he was, but his coaches quickly realized they had an impressive young talent on their hands. Initially, Davies played as a winger: he was incredibly quick, very skilful, a smart dribbler and tactically intelligent. His rise to prominence was astonishing:

At fourteen, Davies joined the youth team of Canadian professional side Vancouver Whitecaps.

At fifteen, he made his MLS (Major League Soccer) debut for Vancouver Whitecaps, playing in a professional league with American and Canadian teams.

At sixteen, he passed a nationality test and was granted Canadian citizenship. On the same day, he was selected for the Canada national team, and he went on to become their youngest ever player.

At seventeen, he signed a contract to join German giants Bayern Munich for a fee of over £8 million.

At eighteen, he scored his first goal for Bayern Munich. He inspired Canada to their first competitive win over rivals USA for 34 years, scoring in a 2–0 win. Canada coach John Herdman says that the rise of Davies shows that "Canada is a country that accepts all".

At nineteen, he was man of the match as Bayern Munich beat Chelsea 3–0 at Stamford Bridge. He set up two goals and was, according to one team-mate, "world-class".

Davies continues to improve in Europe. In his first season at Bayern, he was switched to left-back, and made an immediate impact. His smart positional play helped Bayern's defensive game, while his outrageous speed, as Chelsea found out, was lethal in attack.

Davies is extremely professional and highly motivated. He believes these character traits come from his parents, as they showed in their desire to escape from the civil war and then the refugee camp. "I'm very grateful for everything they've gone through to bring their family to a safe environment and for their kids to have opportunities to be something in the world," Davies said.

His mum Victoria is also proud of how far the whole family, and especially Davies, have come. "When I look back – a refugee camp, no food, no clothes – and here we are today," Victoria said. "Alphonso has everything that he needs. I'm proud of him."

FOOTBALL
MAGAZINE
USA, 2014
"STICK WITH YOUR DREAMS"
Pioneer Pickett inspiring new generation

Carson Pickett was born with her left arm below her elbow missing. It means she does some things differently to others, but it has never stopped her doing anything she wanted to do. She just does things her own way. And that includes her career playing football.

When she was a baby, Pickett found her own way to hold a bottle so she could drink milk. She was given a prosthetic, or artificial, arm when she was six months old, but she threw it across the room. It wasn't long before she found her own way to tie her shoelaces, braid her hair and put on her football kit. When people asked her what it was like to do things with one arm, she would reply: "What's it like to do things with two arms?" She had never known any different. When she was offered an updated prosthetic arm, at the age of eighteen, she turned it down again.

Pickett grew up playing basketball and tennis, as well as swimming competitively. She first played football aged five, and as a left-footer who was exceptionally fast, stood out straightaway. She loved the family atmosphere of being part of a team, and learning about trust and respect. "I love how much sports can teach you about life," she said.

Pickett played for her school team and then was a regular for her Florida State University team. Whenever she found life tough, which she did sometimes, her parents told her she was born for a reason. She was the only person on her team with a physical disability, but it never held her back. Her speed, skill and attitude ensured she developed into one of the best defenders in the country. She was selected for the USA Under-17 and Under-23 teams.

She always dreamed of a professional career. When she was 23, NWSL (National Women's Soccer League) side Seattle Reign signed her. She then moved to Australian side Brisbane Roar before signing for Orlando Pride, where her team-mates included USA World Cup winners Alex Morgan, Ali Krieger and Ashlyn Harris, and Brazilian legend Marta.

Pickett wants her success to show people that disability is not a barrier. "I have the ability to impact a lot of people," she says. "I can use my arm for something greater than myself. To see that I am succeeding in life and happy in life can go a long way for some people. There's always hope if you just stick with your dreams. You're the only one who can stop you from doing what you love."

Pickett wants to share her message with as many people as possible. Shortly after she was born, her parents were introduced to another family whose daughter had a similar disability. Their daughter was older and they reassured the Picketts that their daughter was independent and happy. Pickett is now doing the same thing for others: including a two-year-old boy who supports her team, Orlando Pride.

The pair met after a Pride match, when Pickett went up to the fans behind the goal and saw the little boy, Joseph Tidd. As they bumped arms with each other with huge grins on their faces, the moment was caught on camera; and it went viral. "It was so real and wasn't planned," said Pickett of the photo. "We had an instant bond. It's a gift to feel so much emotion from a little boy who understands you in a way other people can't."

Pickett was commemorated by FIFA in 2019 as a football "Shero" and invited, along with Tidd, to a glitzy awards ceremony. Tidd's father wants Joseph to follow Pickett's example and believe that he can do anything he wants.

Pickett has a tattoo on her right forearm that says: "Imperfection is beauty". Her parents were right: she was born for a reason. She has shown that the way you cope with adversity and treat other people can be powerful and inspiring. As she puts it: "This is something that is much bigger than football."

THE FOOTBALL TIMES

SPECIAL EDITION — USSR, 1943

# Russia's most famous player sent to prison for 10 years

## Spartak star convicted of treason

**Above: Nikolai Starostin now faces a decade behind bars.**

One night in Moscow 1942, the most famous footballer in the Soviet Union, Nikolai Starostin, was woken by a torch shining into his eyes. Two guns were pointing at his head.

It was the secret police. Starostin was under arrest. At the age of forty, he was thrown in jail, where he spent the next year and a half, mostly in solitary confinement.

Starostin had not done anything wrong. But as a well-known sportsman he was an obvious target for the Soviet leader, Joseph Stalin, who ruled over his people by fear. During the 1930s and 1940s, Stalin's government arrested, imprisoned or killed more than a million of its citizens it accused of being enemies.

Starostin, a winger, was a former captain of the national team. He and his three brothers - Aleksandr, Andrey and Pyotr – were the stars of Spartak Moscow, with whom in the late 1930s they twice won the Soviet league and cup double.

The Starostin brothers

After languishing in a Moscow prison, Starostin finally appeared before a judge in 1943 and was sentenced to ten years hard labour. His crime was to have praised the countries of Western Europe. The Soviet Union did not allow freedom of speech, and praising 'enemy' countries was considered a treasonous offence.

Starostin was sent thousands of miles away to serve his sentence, first to a prison camp in the Arctic North and then later one in Siberia. The work was so tough in these camps, and the temperatures so cold, that often inmates died.

But football saved Starostin. The bosses of the camps were football fans and recognized him. They exempted him from work so he could coach the local teams. His fellow prisoners and even the guards treated him like he was a hero.

After five years in the camps, Starostin was again woken up in the night. This time it was a phone call. It was Stalin! Not the leader, but his son, Vasily, who had just become commander in chief of the Soviet Air Force. Vasily wanted Starostin to coach the Air Force's football team, and told Starostin he was sending his personal plane to Siberia to bring him back to Moscow.

Yet even though Starostin was now in favour with Stalin's son, he was still an enemy of the powerful secret police, who wanted to send him back to the camps. For his own safety, Starostin had to stay with Vasily at all times, even sleeping in the same bed, where Vasily hid a gun under the pillow. This situation became impossible and Starostin was eventually exiled to the desert of Kazakhstan, near China and Mongolia.

Stalin died in 1953. A year later, Starostin returned from Kazakhstan to Moscow, and he was allowed to restart his career. He became coach of the Soviet national team, and was made president of Spartak Moscow, a role he held, at first full time and then as an honorary position, until he was 90. He died in 1996 aged 93.

Starostin's misfortune was to be alive during the darkest years of his country's history. No other world-class footballer has ever had to endure what he did. But he kept his self-belief and is now rightly remembered as one of Russia's great sporting heroes.

**EPIC FACTS**

- The Soviet Union (or USSR) was a country that existed between 1922 and 1991, consisting of more than a dozen nations including Russia, Ukraine, Georgia and Kazakhstan.
- Spartak Moscow takes its name from Spartacus, the slave who led the largest slave rebellion in Roman times.

The GOAL
Manchester, 2020
DINNER WINNER
ENGLAND STAR RASHFORD HELPS HUNGRY KIDS

England striker Marcus Rashford spent his time during the coronavirus pandemic doing something far more important than scoring goals. He helped millions of hungry children get free meals when schools were temporarily closed.

There are over one million children in England who rely on eating some of their meals at school every day. Rashford was one of them not so long ago. He grew up in Manchester with four siblings and his mum. Rashford went to a breakfast club in the morning, had a free school lunch then an after-school snack before his mum would cook dinner for the family after coming in late from work.

Rashford went on to become centre-forward for his local team, Manchester United, and became a regular starter for England. As his fame grew, so did his determination to help the next generation of vulnerable children. He worked with a food charity to raise over £20 million, which meant that three million meals a week were delivered to hungry children during the pandemic when schools were closed.

When the government said their meal voucher scheme would stop during the summer holidays, Rashford urged them to reconsider. He wrote an emotional letter, asking, "Can we not all agree that no child should be going to bed hungry?" The government eventually agreed and extended the free meal scheme. "[Combating child poverty is] a trophy [that] stands for something much bigger than football," Rashford said.

By using his platform to highlight such an important message, Rashford has shown that a hero is not just someone who scores lots of goals or performs well on the pitch. It is also someone who thinks of others and tries to make the world a better place.

FOOTBALL
MAGAZINE
Spain, 2018
VINÍCIUS, A
REAL TALENT
The boy
who would
be king

Vinícius Júnior celebrated helping Brazil Under-17s win the 2017 South American championship by taking a selfie of himself clutching his three trophies: one for the tournament victory, the others for top goal-scorer and best player. But his biggest prize came less than a month later: he joined one of the biggest clubs in the world and became one of the most expensive teenagers in football. And he had not even played a professional match in his life!

Vinícius grew up sharing a cramped room with more than half a dozen family members in São Gonçalo, a suburb of Rio de Janeiro notorious for its violent crime and poverty. His family could not always afford the fees to keep him training at a local football club. When he was ten, Flamengo, one of Brazil's most successful clubs, signed Vinícius to its academy. It was on the other side of Rio and his journey sometimes took three hours. A few years later, Vinícius moved in with his uncle Ulysses, who lived nearby.

He was sixteen and still a member of the Flamengo youth academy when he exploded onto the scene in that South American youth championship in March 2017. Playing on the left wing, he scored seven goals in nine games, and was unplayable in the final, in which Brazil beat Chile 5–0.

At the same time as Vinícius's heroics, another Brazilian was making headlines in Europe. Neymar Júnior, after four incredibly successful years at Barcelona, was leaving to join Paris Saint-Germain. Barcelona was desperate for a replacement. Vinícius had already shown superb skill, balance, speed, and daring – even though he had not yet been tested at a higher level.

The shadow of Neymar played a role in what happened next. Barcelona were undeterred by Vinícius's inexperience and bid nearly £8 million for him. That's a lot of money for a player who had never played a professional match! Their rivals Real Madrid had also watched Vinícius star in the South American youth championship; they had also tried and failed to sign Neymar when he was younger. They did not want to miss out on another talented Brazilian youngster. Real Madrid bid more for him. Barcelona came back with a higher bid. Back and forth the bidding went and the money kept increasing. The winning bidder was Real Madrid. The amount they paid for Vinícius was an eye-watering £38 million. The teenager became a millionaire overnight.

There is always risk attached to any new signing a club makes. But with a teenager yet to play at the senior level, there are even more! Some players who excel in the Under-17s are not able to transfer their skills to the higher age group. Some grow faster or stronger at an earlier age and then lose that advantage later. Some get distracted by outside influences and lose their focus; others might end up injured, or with a coach who does not rate them, or in an environment that doesn't inspire them. There are many different factors that go into making a professional footballer, including an element of luck. Everything needs to come together at the right time.

Vinícius spent one more year with Flamengo. When he turned eighteen, in the summer of 2018, he moved to Madrid. In his first two seasons in Spain he showed glimpses of his exceptional talent – including scoring for Real Madrid in the Champions League and in a *clásico* victory against Barcelona. The Madrid coaches remain patient as he is still young and learning a new style of play that is very different to his education in Brazil. They are confident that Vinícius will fulfil his potential.

The boy wonder is doing all he can to make sure that Madrid gets value for money from their incredible decision to sign him. He's a young hero, hoping that his best moments are ahead of him.

## EPIC STATS

Brazil exports more players around the world than any other country. Here are five other Brazilians who moved to Europe as teenagers:

| PLAYER | CLUB JOINED | AGE | FEE |
|---|---|---|---|
| Gabriel Jesus | Man City | 19 | €27m |
| Philippe Coutinho | Inter Milan | 16 | €4m |
| Roberto Firmino | Hoffenheim | 19 | €3.5m |
| David Luiz | Benfica | 19 | €1m |
| Fabinho | Rio Ave | 18 | €750k |

FOOTBALL
MAGAZINE
France, 2016
EURO HERO
Ronaldo inspires
Portugal to glory
7
7

Cristiano Ronaldo has won league titles and Champions League finals. He has broken goal-scoring records and lifted the Ballon D'Or. But his most memorable game is one in which he did not score a dramatic winner or bag a hat-trick. It was the 2016 Euro final, in which Portugal was up against France. The game would become known as "The Ronaldo Final" – but not for the reasons you might expect.

Portugal had never before won an international tournament. Ronaldo was desperate to be successful: not only to secure eternal glory in his home nation, but to steal a march on his great rival Lionel Messi, who had also never won a tournament with his national team. This was an exciting side-drama in their long-running battle to be the world's best.

At the Euros, Portugal was a defensively solid team that relied on Ronaldo's individual brilliance. He was team captain, and had played a huge role in helping Portugal reach the final. His presence had dominated every match; from complaining about Iceland's tactics after the opening-match draw, missing a penalty against Austria and then scoring two goals – one a cheeky backheel – in a 3–3 draw against Hungary.

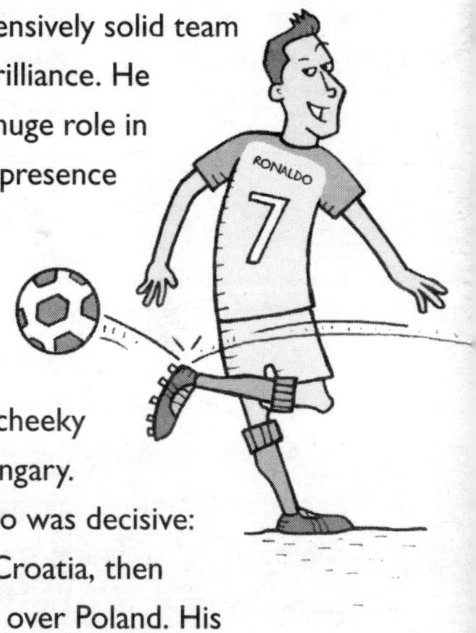


In the knockout matches, Ronaldo was decisive: he set up Portugal's winner against Croatia, then scored in the penalty shoot-out win over Poland. His goal and assist in the semi-final against Wales clinched Portugal's spot in the final. Their opponents were France, the tournament hosts who, with the likes of Hugo Lloris, Paul Pogba and Antoine Griezmann, were expected to win.

Seven minutes into the final. Ronaldo collided with France winger Dmitri Payet, and fell to the ground clutching his knee. The whole of Portugal held its breath. He received treatment and limped back onto the pitch. He could barely walk. He went off again and briefly returned, but with tears in his eyes, he asked the coach to replace him. Ronaldo is brilliant; even a half-fit Ronaldo is better than most players. But a Ronaldo that can't run at all: he had to come off.

And so, in the biggest international match of his career, Ronaldo put the team first. The star player was stretchered off with not even half an hour of the match played. Every Portuguese fan's greatest nightmare had come true; on the biggest stage of all, Ronaldo would not be able to save the day for his nation. Surely Portugal's chances were ruined.

Ronaldo watched the rest of the game, which finished 0–0, from the sidelines. In the period before extra time, he walked around each of his team-mates, urging them to make one last effort towards making history.

As the last thirty minutes of the match played out, Ronaldo became even more animated. He stood next to coach Fernando Santos in the technical area, limping heavily as he bellowed out tactical instructions. He demanded that one player, Raphaël Guerreiro, take a free kick from the edge of the area, but it hit the crossbar. Ronaldo was showing the desire to win that has pushed him to be one of the best players of his generation. It was hard for fans to tell who was the real coach of the team.

The game was decided ten minutes before the end. One of Portugal's substitutes, Eder, hit a low shot from outside the area that fizzed into the corner of the France net. Ronaldo could not have done it better himself!

On the sideline, Ronaldo pumped his fists in excitement. When the final whistle blew, confirming Portugal as European champions, Ronaldo cried again, though this time the tears were of relief, joy and happiness. Ronaldo had dragged Portugal to the final, and his team-mates repaid him in the best way possible.

Ronaldo had broken several individual records during the tournament – including all-time top goal-scorer and appearance-maker, as well as the only player to score in four different tournaments – but winning the final as a team was the only one that mattered to him. He tied a Portugal flag around his waist and hobbled towards the presentation area to lift the trophy. With tears in his eyes, he hoisted aloft the trophy. One of the greatest individual players in the game had helped his country make history.

Home - BOTN News

backofthenet.co.uk/schoolboystuns

News | Fixtures | Teams | Tables

# Schoolboy stuns Manchester United

Manchester

2019

## Matheson back to class after Old Trafford goal

Luke Matheson was just sixteen years old when he scored against Manchester United in a League Cup tie. The teenager was playing for Rochdale against the home side at a packed Old Trafford. But Matheson could not spend long celebrating his amazing achievement: the next day he was back at school to sit a psychology test as part of his A-Level studies!

Matheson was playing as an attacking right-back for Rochdale, a small club that plays in League One (the third division). He had been in and out of the team before he was selected to start against one of England's biggest clubs in September 2019. Rochdale was 1–0 down when his team-mate Ollie Rathbone looped a cross towards the far post. Matheson, who has always been rapid, burst into the area, overtook his marker, and volleyed a shot into the ground and past the goalkeeper.

After the ball hit the net, he ran towards the crowd and slid on his knees. His parents could not believe what they had seen – and nor could his twenty classmates who were also in the stadium. The game finished 1–1 and United won on penalties.

After his United heroics, Matheson, who at the time was in Year 11, said he was determined to complete his A-Levels alongside developing his football career. His school allowed him extra time to complete work around his training schedule.

Matheson was praised for his poise in front of the TV cameras, and his important message that learning comes first. Once he turned seventeen, he hit two more landmarks: he passed his driving test and the very next day, signed a contract to join Wolverhampton Wanderers for £1 million.

He is continuing his studies at his new club, and excited for the opportunities that will follow. As he put it: "I just want to play football and enjoy my education."

The GOAL
London, 1995
SCORPION
IMPOSSIBLE KICK STUNS WORLD

Colombian goalkeeper René Higuita lit up a match against England with an act of acrobatic genius that had never been seen before – or since.

Higuita used to be a prolific striker and was a particularly skilful dribbler. He ended up in goal only by accident, when he filled in between the posts as a teenager after a team-mate was injured. He loved it there! But he also loved dribbling past opponents. He would combine the two by playing on the edge of his area, ready to rush out, dribble past strikers and start his team's attacks.

Higuita was also a showman who loved to entertain the fans. That's exactly what he did when Colombia visited Wembley for a friendly match against England in 1995.

England midfielder Jamie Redknapp tried to lob Higuita from long-range. As the ball looped towards the net, Higuita took one step back and then jumped up, launching himself forward and flicking up his feet behind his back. Somehow, the soles of his feet cleanly connected with the ball. From beneath his own crossbar, horizontal in the air, Higuita cleared the shot away, kicking the ball some distance. It landed outside the area.

No one could quite believe what they had seen! It was only after studying replays that it became clear just how risky and brilliant the move was. Any error of timing would have led to a goal. "The Scorpion Kick", as it quickly became known, turned Higuita into a legend.

Higuita later revealed that he practised the Scorpion Kick for five years before attempting it on the big stage. He was certain that no one would try it again. "Today's goalkeepers do not take risks like I used to," he said.

# THE FOOTBALL TIMES

SPECIAL EDITION | Russia, 2018

## Shepherd goalkeeper is World Cup hero for Iran

### Spot-kick save stuns Portugal

**Above: Beiranvand dives to save Ronaldo's penalty.**

Alireza Beiranvand has travelled further, worked harder and taken more risks than most people to fulfil his dream. His story is a remarkable rise: from living in a tiny village in Iran to making a dramatic impact on the World Cup stage.

His parents were sheep farmers. As the eldest child, he was happy to help his parents and Beiranvand spent much of his childhood moving to wherever there was enough grass for the sheep. Whenever he had free time, he would play with his friends; either football or Dal Paran, a game in which you need to throw stones a long way.

Beiranvand dreamed of being a goalkeeper, but the shepherd's life was not the ideal preparation. In fact, it was a huge disadvantage; the family was constantly on the move while fighting to survive drought and dust storms. His father, Morteza, wanted Beiranvand to focus on farming and even tore his goalkeeper gloves in the hope it would stop him from playing. Instead, he just kept goal with bare hands.

When he was a teenager, Beiranvand ran away to the capital city Tehran, in the hope of finding a club to play for. On the bus heading to the city, he met a football coach who promised to train him. Beiranvand did not have any money, or anywhere to stay, so he slept outside the football club's front door. We don't advise this!

Beiranvand took on a succession of jobs while he trained as a goalkeeper. He worked in a dressmaking factory, a pizzeria and a car wash. Once, he cleaned the car of Iran's most famous footballer, Ali Daei, scorer of a record 109 goals for the national team. He was too embarrassed to ask for help with his football career. "If I had talked to Mr Daei he would have surely helped me but I was ashamed to tell him about my situation," he said.

Beiranvand soon signed for a Tehran team called Naft, and his skills went viral following a game in November 2014. He jumped to catch a cross against rival team Tractor, and ran to the edge of his area to pass the ball. He spotted the Naft centre-forward running into space in the opposition half and he hurled the ball towards him. The ball zoomed through the air, bouncing around 70 metres away. It fell into the striker's path perfectly; with his first touch, he fired the ball into the corner of the net. Beiranvand was able to throw the ball huge distances with unerring accuracy. All that time playing Dal Paran had paid off!

Within one year, Beiranvand was Iran's first-choice goalkeeper. He kept twelve clean sheets in qualifying matches to help Iran qualify for the 2018 World Cup.

Then came the moment that must have surpassed Beiranvand's wildest dreams: in a group match against Portugal in the 2018 World Cup in Russia, Iran, already one goal down, conceded a penalty. Portugal captain, Cristiano Ronaldo, stepped up to shoot. The world was watching as the superstar faced the shepherd. As Ronaldo struck the ball, Beiranvand leapt to his left. The ball seemed to follow him and it landed in his gloves. Beiranvand saved the spot kick! Iran went on to score a late goal to achieve a creditable 1–1 draw and Beiranvand was the hero for Iran.

"I suffered many difficulties to make my dreams come true but I have no intention of forgetting them because they made me the person I am now," he said. After all the obstacles he overcame to reach his dream, the humble shepherd deserved his moment in the spotlight

**EPIC FACT**

Beiranvand was in goal for a match that made history in October 2019, when Iran beat Cambodia 14–0 in a World Cup qualifier. The result was irrelevant: it was the first time in 40 years that Iran's government had allowed women to watch qualifying matches of a football tournament. The decision came after years of protests by women standing up for their rights. Beiranvand was also overjoyed – one of the women watching was his wife.

Home - BOTN News ×

← → C backofthenet.co.uk/sinclairsmashesscoringrecord

News | Fixtures | Teams | Tables

USA

2020

# Sinclair smashes scoring record

## Canadian is greatest striker of all time

Christine Sinclair has never won a World Cup, appeared in an Olympic final or played in the Champions League. Her name is barely spotted on the back of any football jerseys. Yet in January 2020, when the Canada striker escaped her marker and rolled the ball beyond the St Kitts and Nevis goalkeeper and into the back of the net, she made history.

Sinclair had tears in her eyes as she pumped her fists and hugged her team-mates. She had just broken the record for the most goals ever scored in international football. This strike was goal number 185. That's 185 goals! Sinclair is the greatest international goal-scorer of all time, even though she is barely known outside Canada.

Sinclair's achievement took her nearly twenty years – 7,260 days, to be exact – and 290 international games (another record) to accomplish. Sinclair bagged her first goal for Canada aged sixteen, and scored for Canada in each of the next twenty years. How's that for consistency? Two of her team-mates on the pitch during her record-breaking match had not even been born when Sinclair scored her first international goal.

When Sinclair was eighteen, a comment from Canada coach Even Pellerud surprised her. During a pre-match team-talk, Pellerud reminded the team that they had the world's best player. Sinclair looked around as she wasn't sure who he was talking about. Then she saw everyone looking at her! She decided to prove Pellerud right.

**EPIC STAT**

**41**

Number of different teams Sinclair scored her 185 goals against. Her biggest hauls were against Mexico (16 goals), China (12 goals) and the USA (11 goals).

Many experts believe she succeeded in her ambition. Her natural talent helped but she worked hard, stayed fit and kept on improving. Despite that, she was regularly overlooked for major awards – most surprisingly in 2012, when she scored 23 goals in 22 international games. Three of those came in a thrilling 2012 Olympics semi-final defeat against USA. Sinclair had put Canada ahead three times, and three times USA equalized (Megan Rapinoe scored twice, once direct from a corner) before sneaking a last-minute extra-time winner to break Canada hearts. At the end of that year, she only finished fifth in the voting for FIFA's Player of the Year. She never finished any higher than that, despite her achievements.

Why was a player of her talents overlooked in this way? First, Sinclair is not an extrovert personality who enjoys the spotlight and wants to have the focus on her. Rather, she is quiet, humble and hard-working. She does not draw attention to herself.

She also plays for Canada, which is a smaller country when it comes to football success than the USA or some European countries. Canada's best ever world ranking is number four, and best tournament finishes have been bronze at the Olympics (in 2012 and 2016) and fourth place in the World Cup (2003). Whether it's fair or not, you are more likely to win individual awards if your team wins trophies.

Sinclair has never played in a European league. Instead she has played exclusively in North America, for five different teams during a time when women's professional leagues were badly run and set up by three separate organizations. The rise to prominence of one of her former club team-mates, the Brazilian Marta, was partly because she spent much of her career in Europe.

After her record-breaking goal, Sinclair's team-mates all put on goat masks to represent what they think of her. GOAT is an acronym that stands for Greatest of all Time. True to form, Sinclair was embarrassed by the fuss! Despite that, she is seen as one of Canada's greatest athletes and has inspired a generation of young footballers.
Will anyone ever be able to break her record?

The GOAL
Argentina, 1985
SLEEPING BEAUTY
COACH SCOUTS SNORING SUPERSTAR
ZZZZ

One of the strangest signings in football history began in the dead of night. Two strangers were driving through Murphy, a small town in the north-east of Argentina, looking to sign a teenage footballer. The year was 1985 and the strangers were Marcelo Bielsa and Jorge Griffa. At the time, they were youth coaches working for Newell's Old Boys, a top-division club that was on the hunt for new players.

The pair stopped at a service station and asked where they might find the house of a particular family. Murphy is a small place, so someone was able to tell them where this boy, then aged thirteen, lived. The coaches had been tipped off by a local scout that this youngster was a decent player. By the time they eventually found the house, it was two o'clock in the morning.

Rather than wait until the next morning, the pair knocked on the door and woke up the boy's mother, Amalia. She went to wake up her husband, Hector. He had heard of the pair and asked them to come in. They drank coffee and explained the purpose of their visit; that they were looking for talent and had heard of their son. Once they had run out of small talk, Griffa asked, "Could we see the boy?"

He was, of course, fast asleep. Despite the strange request, his parents agreed and they all went into the bedroom to see the sleeping boy. Griffa then had another, even stranger request. "May I see his legs?" he asked. His mother pulled the covers off his legs and the coaches leaned forward, excited about what they might find. Even though his parents were present and allowed this to happen, it was still a bizarre request! It was as though the coaches were examining the legs of a thoroughbred racehorse in the stables rather than a boy.

The coaches then said nine words that would change the life of the sleeping teenager: "He looks like a footballer! Look at those legs!"

What had they spotted that was so special? Was it the length of his limbs, or their thickness? Were his calf muscles visible, or was there some unseen skill they could detect in his toes? To this day, no one knows for sure.

But one thing was certain: Marcelo Bielsa would become one of the most influential coaches in football history, famous for his attention to detail. But no decision was as strange as the one he made in that player's bedroom. Based on the sleeping boy's legs, he said he wanted him to go to Newell's for a trial.

The next morning, over breakfast, the boy's mother told him that the two coaches had visited him when he was fast asleep. He did not believe her, accusing her of dreaming it.

Still, he went for the trial. Bielsa wanted to see the boy at centre-back, a position he had never played before. He was on the pitch for five minutes, and had only touched the ball three or four times, when the coach took him off. Bielsa had seen enough. He wanted to sign him. And so he did.

It turned out to be an incredible decision. Bielsa and his new player helped Newell's win the 1991 Argentinian title (this is why the Newell's home ground is now called the Marcelo Bielsa Stadium). Bielsa's success grew and he coached in Mexico and Spain before being appointed head coach of Argentina. For the 2002 World Cup, he picked the boy he had scouted when he was asleep.

Bielsa was such an influential coach that many players in his squad went on to become successful coaches themselves, including Diego Simeone, who won Spain's league title with Atletico Madrid, and Marcelo Gallardo, twice a Copa Libertadores champion with River Plate.

But what happened to that player from Murphy, the one who was scouted while he was asleep and who only needed five minutes of his trial to convince the coach he had what it takes? Well, he also became a successful coach. His name? Mauricio Pochettino.

Home - BOTN News ×

backofthenet.co.uk/fansweepforstar

News | Fixtures | Teams | Tables

The Netherlands

2017

# Fans weep for star

## Ajax prodigy in near-death collapse

Dutch winger Abdelhak Nouri was tipped to be one of the world's best players when in 2017, aged only twenty, he suffered a heart attack playing for Ajax during a pre-season friendly. His team-mates were horrified to watch Appie, as they called him, slip into unconsciousness. He was taken to hospital but doctors could not revive him, and he stayed in a coma for nearly three years. Yet even though Nouri's football career was over, his impact was felt across the Netherlands.

Nouri had broken into Ajax's first team one year earlier and was destined to become the next superstar from the club's famous academy. He was a popular figure throughout the country and not just because he played for one of the Netherlands' biggest teams. It was because of how he behaved off the pitch too.

His father, Mohammed Nouri, had originally come from Morocco to settle in the north-east town of Geuzenveld. His son was at the heart of this busy migrant community. After his heart attack, players and fans came together to share their memories of how Nouri would enjoy a kickabout with people from the town, often picking disabled kids to be on his side. He would visit people who had suffered a death in the family; help locals pay for groceries; and, as a school ambassador, encourage youngsters to study hard.

After his tragic collapse, banners declaring "Stay Strong Appie" and "Appie 4 Ever" appeared across the Netherlands. In his darkest moment, Nouri's influence on his community was greater than ever. Thousands of fans from around the world visited Geuzenveld to pay their respects outside his house and show their love, with an emotional outpouring that united everyone, not just Ajax fans. People came from Morocco, Singapore and even China to show their support.

One photographer who was present when Nouri's grieving father, Mohammed, acknowledged the huge crowd outside his house, described the moment: "All the visible and invisible divisions separating people in the city suddenly melted away." That was the power Nouri had.

Nouri received regular visits from his Ajax team-mates. His best friend, Frenkie de Jong, made a special trip in summer 2019 to tell him he was joining Barcelona. Nouri could have been his team-mate there one day. Many former team-mates from the Ajax youth team wore his shirt number, 34, for the next season, to honour their friend.

When Ajax won the Dutch league title in 2019, they dedicated the victory to Nouri and invited his father Mohammed to join in the celebrations. The victory was all the more poignant because it was title number 34 in the club's history.

Although Nouri's family were told by doctors that he would never recover, they believed otherwise. Nearly three years later, in 2020, he woke up from his coma. Today, he is still bedridden but, according to his brother Abderrahim, he can eat, sneeze, smile – and burp! His family involves him in their conversations and he can communicate yes or no using his eyebrows. They all enjoy watching football together. The family has set up a charity in his name to help other people with disabilities. Nouri's story is one that brings sadness, but also powerful hope.

**EPIC FACT**

Former France defender Jean-Pierre Adams had an operation on his knee in 1982 and never woke up from it. He has been in a coma for over 38 years, the longest any man has been in a prolonged state of unconsciousness. His wife Bernadette looks after him every day, feeding him liquidized food, in a customized house that she calls *Mas du Bel Athléte Dormant*, The House of the Beautiful Sleeping Athlete.

FOOTBALL
MAGAZINE
Liverpool, 2020
SPEEDO SUPERSTAR
Everton fan raises
fortune in his trunks
Everton

When it comes to watching his team play, Michael Cullen doesn't need to think about what to wear. The 55-year-old Everton fan puts on the same outfit for every match: sturdy hiking boots, a pair of Everton swimming trunks – and a big smile! Nothing else! Sometimes Cullen gets chilly, but he says the affectionate response he gets from fellow fans warms him up nicely. This unique football fan is one cool customer.

Speedo Mick, as he is known, earned his nickname when he swam across the English Channel to France in 2016. He wore Everton swimming trunks for that challenge and he has barely taken them off since. In 2019, wearing only swimming trunks (and sometimes an Everton scarf and bobble hat), he conquered freezing cold temperatures, torrential rain and a painful calf injury to walk 1,000 miles and raise thousands of pounds for charity.

He started his trek at the UK's northernmost point, John O'Groats in Scotland, and walked to its southernmost point, Land's End in Cornwall. He needed medical treatment for his calf along the way – and so stopped off at Everton's training ground for a session with the club physio and some encouragement from the players. He admitted that doing the walk during winter was challenging. Brrrr!

In his past, Speedo Mick was homeless and addicted to alcohol. He is now trying to help others who find themselves in similar difficult situations. Speedo Mick's fundraising efforts have helped to fund a local hospice and raised thousands to help Everton's community projects. That makes this trunks-man superfan an epic hero!

Home - BOTN News ×

backofthenet.co.uk/blindfaith

News | Fixtures | Teams | Tables

# Blind faith

Spain

2020

## Superfan immortalized after death

Vicente Navarro was one of Spanish club Valencia's biggest fans. When he went blind aged 54, he continued to go to every home match at Valencia's Mestalla stadium with his son, who explained the action unfolding on the pitch for him. Navarro moved his seat from the centre-line so he could be closer to the pitch and hear the action better. For over 30 years, he sat in Seat 164 of Row 15 in the Tribuna Central section.

Twenty years after Navarro lost his sight, Valencia won the Spanish league title in 2004. Navarro said it was the happiest year of his life! Soon after, they won the Spanish Cup. His son, also called Vicente, said: "Dad wanted to feel the club."

Navarro had a watch that spoke the time when he pressed a button. Superstitious fans watching around him trusted his watch more than the referee's timekeeping; they would tell him to press the button when they were getting tense before the end of matches.

Navarro had been excited to celebrate the 2019 season, the club's 100th anniversary. Sadly, however, he died in 2016, at the age of 88. Valencia did not want their superfan to miss the party – or any future games, though. They built a bronze statue which permanently occupies Seat 164, Row 15 of Tribuna Central. "He is a symbol who represents, forever, all those who experienced the emotion of supporting Valencia," said the club.

In 2020, when the coronavirus pandemic forced some matches in Europe to be played in empty stadiums, Valencia played a Champions League knockout match against Atalanta. They lost the game 3–4 and no fans were in the stadium to see it. Except one. Navarro's statue was there, in Seat 164, Row 15 of Tribuna Central. Just like always.

FOOTBALL
MAGAZINE
Glasgow, 2011
THISTLE SHOW 'EM!
Lottery win funds
Scottish minnows

What would you do if you won the lottery? Move to a new house, take an exciting holiday, donate to charity, or maybe buy some cool new trainers? Colin Weir was a TV cameraman when he scooped the biggest amount ever won in the EuroMillions lottery in 2011: an astonishing £161.6 million. Weir was determined to spend his money wisely, saying: "With great wealth comes great responsibility." So he bought his favourite football team!

Partick Thistle is a small team based in west Glasgow. It has never won the league title in the top division, but it did win the Scottish Cup, back in 1921. The two biggest clubs in Glasgow are Celtic and Rangers, with Thistle a distant third. Yet Thistle was the team that Weir had followed for his whole life – and he was desperate to help them.

Weir was sensible with how he used his funds. He did not plough the money into signing new players who might not work out, but instead he worked to protect the future of the club. He paid off all the debts that Thistle owed to the bank, and funded a youth academy with a £2.5 million payment to ensure the club could produce great young talent to keep it sustainable.

The Thistle Weir Youth Academy, as it is known, quickly earned back on the investment, by selling exciting young players to clubs in England. The club developed a successful women's football programme. Weir also promised to spend another £6 million on a new state-of-the-art training centre.

Weir died in 2019, but before he passed away, he made sure the club was in safe hands. A group of fans called Thistle For Ever wanted to run the club for the community. So Weir gave them his ownership of the club as a gift! "Fans talk about Thistle being their club – and now it really will be," he said.

Home - BOTN News ×

backofthenet.co.uk/thaifootballteam

News | Fixtures | Teams | Tables

Thailand

2018

# Thai football team rescued from cave

## Boys safe after nine days without food or light

A junior football team and their football coach were rescued after spending seventeen days without food or light in a cave in Thailand. The daring rescue attempt, led by elite Navy SEALs and international diving experts, took three days and gripped millions around the world.

The dramatic story began after football practice one Saturday in June 2018. The Wild Boars football team and their coach, Ake, cycled to the Tham Luang cave. The network of narrow tunnels and chambers wind for several miles under the ground and is a tourist attraction in the north of Thailand. The team left their bikes at the cave's entrance and took off their football boots. They had all been to the cave before, so took with them only their torches, some water and a few snacks.

After an hour's exploring, the team realized that the cave chamber they were in was quickly filling up with water and there was no way out. They escaped from the rising water to a dry, sandy spot and sat down to spend the night inside the cave.

At first, their coach wasn't too worried. He thought that they would be rescued in the morning. He made the boys huddle together to stay warm. But no one came the next day. No one came the day after, or the day after that. Soon the group lost all track of time and once their torch batteries ran out, they were left in complete darkness. A week passed and the boys were still trapped. They licked the wet cave walls for water, but there was nothing to eat. Everyone felt faint and tired.

Inside the cave, the boys had no idea that they had become the most famous football team in the world. Their parents had rushed to the cave when they didn't return home, found their bikes and boots and raised the alarm. The race to find the Wild Boars was quickly followed by TV stations, news websites and newspapers first in Thailand and then across the globe. No one knew if the boys were alive or dead.

The rescue operation began the day after the boys went missing. The challenge was to work out where the boys might be in the cave network. Thai Navy SEALs faced freezing cold water, strong currents and narrow tunnels and, of course, it was pitch black. Expert cave divers from many other countries made their way to Tham Luang to offer their help. After a week, the Wild Boars were the biggest news story in the world.

By the tenth day, many people had lost hope that the Wild Boars would be found alive. Then two British divers popped out of the water in a chamber more than a mile underground. The divers' torches lit up thirteen skinny people wearing football kit sitting in the dark. Against the odds, Ake and the boys were all still alive.

When the footage from the divers' cameras was released, everyone was ecstatic that the boys had been found. However it was going to be very risky to get the team out safely. Even the experienced divers had found the tunnels difficult to swim through. Divers brought the boys food and clothes while they worked out a plan.

The operation began a week later. Each boy was given an oxygen mask and strapped to a stretcher, which was guided by an experienced diver. It took one hundred people three days to get them all out of the cave. The families of the boys – and the rest of the world – were overjoyed to see the Wild Boars re-emerge from darkness after their seventeen-day ordeal.

The fact that they survived was a miracle. "This experience taught me to value my life," said one of the boys afterwards. "This event has made me stronger."

**EPIC FACT**

A Thai Navy diver died during the rescue operation when his tanks ran out of air. The boys promised the diver's family that, to honour his memory, they would spend nine days in a Buddhist monastery. A year later they kept their promise and were ordained as novice monks.

Home - BOTN News

backofthenet.co.uk/tacticalgenius

News | Fixtures | Teams | Tables

# Tactical genius

Germany

2019

## Top club hires unknown blogger

René Marić was obsessed with football and loved talking about it with his friends. He lived in a small village in Austria and when he was still a teenager he coached a local Under-17 team. He also worked with an amateur team where he coached players aged between 15 and 44. Marić got on well with everyone and enjoyed helping teams reach their full potential.

Marić wanted to share his thoughts about the game with people beyond his village. With four friends, he set up a blog dedicated to football tactics. The blog was written in German and called *Spielverlagerung*, which translates as 'Match movement' in English. Anyone can set up a blog, and Marić hoped that a few fellow football fanatics, or maybe amateur coaches, would read it and discuss their shared passion. But that wasn't quite how it worked out.

A professional coach found his website and read it. That coach was Thomas Tuchel, who at the time was coaching Mainz in the Bundesliga, the German top division. He was impressed with how Marić had described his team's tactics against Bayern Munich. Tuchel, who went on to coach Borussia Dortmund and Paris Saint-Germain, asked Marić to help him analyse opposition tactics before matches.

Tuchel was not the only one who wanted Marić's insights. Marić did some analysis for Brentford, the English club. A coach called Marco Rose also read Marić's blog when he was working with RB Salzburg's Under-18 team. Rose, who when he was a player had Jürgen Klopp as his coach, met with Marić many times to talk about his articles and the pair became friends. When Rose was promoted to coach the Under-19s, he asked Marić to become his assistant coach. Marić said yes. Well, wouldn't you? He stopped blogging and started coaching!

In their first season together, the team played in the UEFA Youth League, a youth version of the Champions League. Inspired by Marić's tactical insight, RB Salzburg's youngsters were victorious against Manchester City, Paris Saint-Germain and Barcelona before beating Benfica 2–1 in the final. They became the first Austrian side to ever win a European trophy.

Before long, Rose and Marić were promoted to coach RB Salzburg's first team. At first, there was some surprise that Marić, who was only 24 at the time, younger than many of the players in his squad, was there. But once the team started playing, no one complained. They were brilliant! More success followed.

RB Salzburg won the Austrian league in their first season and again impressed in Europe. RB Salzburg beat big teams like Borussia Dortmund and Lazio to reach the Europa League semi-final. Big clubs around Europe began to notice that Rose and his bright assistant were outsmarting their opponents with clever tactics and exciting football. After RB Salzburg won the Austrian league and Cup double in their second season, another opportunity emerged.

This time it was in the Bundesliga, where Marić's adventure had first begun. Borussia Mönchengladbach is one of Germany's most successful clubs; only Bayern Munich has won the league title more times. In 2019, they appointed Rose and Marić to turn the team around, which is exactly what they did. Borussia Mönchengladbach challenged for the Bundesliga title for the first time in decades.

The pair are among Europe's most exciting young coaches today. Klopp himself has tipped Rose for the top – and you can expect Marić to join him on the way. Not every football hero scores the winning goal or prowls the technical area shouting at players. What started off for Marić as a hobby with his friends has turned into a professional coaching career. And the journey for this tactics wizard is only just beginning.

# FOOTBALL
MAGAZINE

France, 2005

## POO-TIFUL GAME

Smelly secrets of football's longest-serving coach

Guy Roux was 22 when he applied for the job of head coach at an amateur fourth-division French team called Auxerre. Because he wasn't asking for very much money, he got the job. That happened back in 1961. Roux went on to stay in the job until 2005, an astonishing FORTY-FOUR years. In that time, he ended up leading Auxerre to the French first division title and the dizzying heights of the Champions League.

As Auxerre was an amateur side when Roux was first appointed, they did not have much money. Roux was in charge of everything, and needed to be creative in finding solutions. So he persuaded local farmers to donate their goats' poo to help grow Auxerre's training pitches, he asked his players' wives to make bibs for training and in the evenings he would answer the club's phones as no one else was around.

Roux coached Auxerre for around 2,000 games, almost half of which were in the first division. Roux's Auxerre team reached the first division in 1980 and won the league title in 1996. By then, he was one of the most famous men in France.

Some of the players who came through his academy went on to have great careers and play for France, including Djibril Cissé, Eric Cantona and Basile Boli. Roux could spot a talented player, but also knew how to get the best out of them. He also had a reputation for being tough on his players: he demanded total dedication to the team.

Auxerre struggled when Roux left the club. They were relegated a few years later and have remained in the second division ever since. "To be a manager, you need two things," Roux said. "To be an example, and to love your players."

The GOAL

Gabon, 2012

# FROM GRIEF TO GLORY

## ZAMBIA ARE FINALLY AFRICAN CHAMPS

When Zambia reached the final of the Africa Cup of Nations in 2012, the moment was bittersweet for the country. The Zambians were poised to win their first ever African title, their greatest sporting triumph, yet the country was still grieving from a plane crash two decades before in which eighteen players from the national team died.

The crash in 1993 took the lives of a golden generation of Zambian players. The Zambian Football Federation took years to build a new team, always in the shadow of the one that was lost. But in 2012, against the odds, a young Zambia team of unknowns reached the final of the Africa Cup of Nations (the African equivalent of the Euros).

By strange coincidence, the final was in Libreville, the capital of Gabon, only a few miles from the site of the 1993 crash. On the day before the final, the players visited the crash site to pay their respects. They all laid down flowers and sang the team song.

The final was against overwhelming favourites Côte d'Ivoire, who had several players from the top European leagues. Yet remarkably, Zambia, nicknamed the Copper Bullets, held on as the match finished 0–0, after Côte d'Ivoire missed a second-half penalty.

The game went to a penalty shoot-out, and it was one of the longest and most dramatic shoot-outs in the history of international football.

During the shoot-out, a line of around twenty Zambian squad members, made up of substitutes and backroom staff, sang the team song in unison. The Zambia players in the centre-circle, some waiting to take the single most important kick in their lives, joined in. It was an emotional atmosphere; the song linked the memory of the tragic past team to the current side on the verge of success. The noise from the fans in the packed stadium added to the tension.

Both teams scored their first seven kicks, then missed the next one. On the next kick, Gervinho, the Côte d'Ivoire striker, hit his penalty over the bar. The chance to win the game for Zambia fell to Stoppila Sunzu. A defender, Sunzu was three years old when the 1993 team perished. As he walked to the spot, he carried on singing the team song. He spotted the ball, stepped backwards to his mark and was still singing.

"We had thought how wonderful it would be to win the Cup for the nation," Sunzu said. "You just have to know where to place the ball and if you strike it well, you will score even if the goalkeeper dives the right way."

And so, nineteen years and just a few miles from the site of a tragedy that wiped out a whole team and devastated a nation, Sunzu channelled the power of song, prayer and belief to score his penalty and make the winning score 8–7. It was one of the greatest surprise results in African football.

**EPIC FACT**

Zambia is home to the Victoria Falls, the world's largest natural waterfall and one of the Seven Natural Wonders of the World. Zambians call the waterfall Mosi-oa-Tunya, which means "The smoke that thunders". The noise of the water can be heard from 25 miles away. Loud!

Zambia, finally, had won the Africa Cup of Nations. A country that had suffered unbearable tragedy was united again: this time in joyful triumph.

The GOAL
Germany, 2020
MEDITATION INSPIRATION
COMPOSURE KEY TO HAALAND SUCCESS
BVB 09

Erling Braut Haaland has broken goal-scoring records wherever he has played. Haaland comes from a talented family, as his father, Alf-Inge Haaland, was a former Leeds and Manchester City midfielder who played for Norway. The younger Haaland was born in Leeds and dreamed of a career in football. No one knew how quickly he would emulate his dad!

Alf-Inge retired when Haaland was three years old and the family returned to western Norway. Haaland joined a local club, Bryne, when he was five and quickly impressed his coaches. Even at that age, he was always willing to work hard and learn.

Haaland was one of the best players, but the coaches picked teams with mixed abilities so it was rare that all the best players were on the same team. That meant Haaland was always inventing new tricks to win games, in order make up for the fact that his team-mates were not as good as him. Over the next ten years, he never moved to a professional academy as he enjoyed playing with his friends. His team would have one training session and a match during the week, and weekends were free to play on an indoor pitch with friends. He did this all weekend! Every weekend! Well, wouldn't you?

Haaland was a small kid whose growth spurt came when he turned fourteen. Before then, he had to rely on movement, speed and intelligence to find space from his markers. Those skills would come in useful before long.

Haaland started playing against adults when he was fifteen, when he made his senior debut in Norway's first division for Bryne in 2016. Within a year, he joined a bigger team, Molde, where he scored twenty goals in fifty games. Then he moved to Austrian champions RB Salzburg, where he scored at a rate of more than one goal per game.

By now he was a regular in Norway's youth teams. In May 2019, he played in the Under-20 World Cup and made history with nine goals in a 12–0 win over Honduras. Haaland hit a triple hat-trick – a hat-trick of hat-tricks! As he came off the pitch, he said: "I think I should have scored ten. It's a shame, but in the end I'm happy with nine."

Manchester United tried to sign him in January 2020, but Haaland moved to German side Borussia Dortmund. It did not take long to realize it was a good decision: Haaland came off the bench on his debut and scored another hat-trick in twenty minutes. He scored two goals on his Champions League debut for Dortmund against Paris Saint-Germain. Never mind eclipsing Alf-Inge Haaland, the teenage striker was outshining Neymar and Kylian Mbappé!

## HAA-PY DAYS

Erling Haaland scored ten goals in his first seven Champions League matches, quicker than any other player in history. Here's how long it took other star players to score ten Champions League goals:

| PLAYER | GAMES |
|---|---|
| Kylian Mbappé | 15 |
| Robert Lewandwoski | 17 |
| Lionel Messi | 23 |
| Sergio Agüero | 26 |
| Cristiano Ronaldo | 31 |

Haaland won extra praise after that PSG game. He meditates before matches to feel calm and, after scoring his goals, Haaland celebrated with a meditation pose: crossed legs, arms outstretched, eyes closed, thumb and middle finger touching. When PSG won the return game, Neymar and all his PSG team-mates copied his celebration. People thought the French team, with Neymar as the ringleader, were teasing Haaland but the Norwegian, then only nineteen, did not react. "They helped me a lot to get meditation out in the world and to show the whole world that meditation is an important thing so I'm thankful that they helped me," he said.

That mature response left observers even more convinced that he is heading for the top. He has rapid pace, remarkable strength and a powerful left foot. Other elements of his game, like his positional play, close control and aerial game are improving fast. Most importantly, Haaland has a champion work ethic and responds well to adversity. This young Norwegian is on the fast-track to becoming one of the best strikers in the world.

# QUIZ

1. **Which of the following did Biriba do before every Botafogo match, because the club boss believed it brought good luck?**

    a) Pooed in the goalmouth
    b) Peed on a player's leg
    c) Licked the referee's nose
    d) Ate grass from the centre-circle

2. **Which England star has helped Olympique Lyonnais Féminin become one of the greatest sports sides in history?**

    a) Ellen White
    b) Steph Houghton
    c) Lucy Bronze
    d) Millie Bright

3. **Complete the puzzling phrase that Eric Cantona said after his ban for kung-fu kicking a fan: "When the seagulls follow the trawler, it's because…"**

    a) "… they need to do a poo."
    b) "… there are no more fish and chips on the shore."
    c) "… they think it's tea-time."
    d) "… they think sardines will be thrown into the sea."

4. **What birdy nickname did Chile captain Roberto Rojas have before he was banned from football for cheating against Brazil?**

    a) Flamingo
    b) Eagle
    c) Sparrow
    d) Condor

5. **Why was the film made about the greatest moment in Bournemouth's history called *Minus 17*?**

    a) They were deducted 17 points and still survived.
    b) That's how cold it was when Bournemouth played.
    c) Coach Eddie Howe was 17 years younger than the next-youngest coach in the division.
    d) They won 17–0.

6. **What was Nicolas de Staël inspired to create after watching France play Sweden in 1952?**

   a) A painting, which later sold for £17 million
   b) A brand new France kit
   c) The first musical ever written about football
   d) A referee's whistle that played the Marseillaise

7. **What did the Bhutanese football federation buy every player in the team who took part in their historic 1–0 victory against Sri Lanka?**

   a) A chicken bucket from KFC
   b) A car
   c) A framed shirt
   d) A holiday to Sri Lanka

8. **Brazilian midfielder Formiga takes her name from which insect that is hard-working and unselfish?**

   a) Beetle
   b) Mosquito
   c) Ant
   d) Earwig

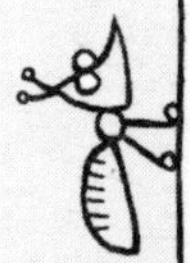

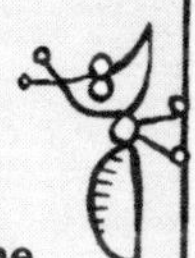

9. **Spain midfielder Ana Romero worked as a doctor during the coronavirus pandemic after getting a degree in what subject?**

   a) Sports science
   b) Medicine
   c) Contagious diseases
   d) Driving ambulances

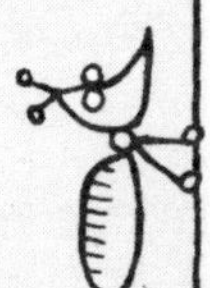

10. **What was unique about how Sunderland beat Liverpool in the Premier League in 2009?**

   a) Every Sunderland player scored in an 11–0 win.
   b) The Sunderland goalkeeper scored a hat-trick.
   c) The entire Liverpool team were sent off.
   d) The winning goal was scored after the ball hit a beach ball on the pitch.

**11. Why was goalkeeper Petr Čech born with a thinner-than-average skull?**

a) His mother had a thinner-than-average skull.
b) He fell over as a child and that damaged his skull.
c) He was one of triplets.
d) He was bald.

**12. What pre-match meal did Arsenal have before beating Liverpool to win the league title on the final day of the season in 1989?**

a) Toast and honey
b) Chicken and pasta
c) Steak and chips
d) Fish and broccoli

**13. What fate awaited Son Heung-min if South Korea had lost the Asian Games final in 2018?**

a) The sack from his club side Tottenham Hotspur
b) His mum grounding him for a month
c) 21 months military service in the Korean army
d) Immediate retirement from football

**14. From where did doctors take muscles to repair Santi Cazorla's damaged Achilles tendon?**

a) Ear
b) Bum
c) Forearm
d) Hamstring

**15. How does Jürgen Klopp describe his tactical football plan?**

a) Classic counter
b) Mega movement
c) Pass and shoot
d) Heavy metal

**16. A book about what profession inspired Rose Lavelle to change her preparation regime and helped her become a World Cup winner?**

a) Accountants
b) Astronauts
c) Farmers
d) Ballet dancers

**17. What was the catchphrase of Leicester City coach Claudio Ranieri in 2016, the season they won the Premier League title?**

a) "I'm a silver fox and I wear blue socks!"
b) "Jamie Vardy's having a party!"
c) "Kick it short, never long!"
d) "Dilly-ding, dilly-dong!"

**18. At the 1971 women's World Cup in Mexico, an injury-hit England team was forced to play three players who were not in the squad for the game against France. They were:**

a) The coach and two of his friends
b) Three fans
c) Three players flown in for the match
d) Three Mexican players

**19. What was special about ten of the players in Celtic's Lisbon Lions team that won the 1967 European Cup final?**

a) They were all related to each other.
b) They all grew up supporting Rangers.
c) They were all left-footed.
d) They were born within ten miles from Celtic's stadium.

**20. What food did world record throw-in champion Thomas Grønnemark spit on his hands to get the best grip?**

a) Sticky rice
b) Liquorice
c) Prunes
d) Sticky toffee pudding

**21. What two rival countries do girlfriends Pernille Harder and Magda Eriksson play for?**

a) Brazil and Argentina
b) USA and Mexico
c) Denmark and Sweden
d) England and Scotland

**22. When Real Madrid won the European Cup in 1960, its striker Alfredo Di Stéfano became the first player to score what?**

a) A goal in five consecutive European Cup finals
b) A goal and an own-goal in a European Cup final
c) A goal against a team he used to play for in a European Cup final
d) Four goals in a European Cup final

**23. What excuse did midfielder Tomás Carlovich give for missing his only call-up to the Argentina national team?**

a) He went fishing and the river flooded.
b) His dog ate his football boots.
c) His bus broke down on the way to training.
d) He overslept as he was dreaming of scoring a hat-trick.

**24. Who did Megan Rapinoe upset before the biggest game of her career at the 2019 World Cup in France?**

a) Her twin sister Rachael
b) Her coach Jill Ellis
c) US President Trump
d) The French fans

**25. Why did Pep Guardiola call Lionel Messi into his office late on the night before Barcelona played Real Madrid?**

a) To explain the new position he would be playing in the next day
b) To inspire with him videos of his greatest goals so far
c) To give him a new cuddly teddy to help him get to sleep
d) To test him on his knowledge of the Madrid defenders

**26. How many goals and assists did Vivianne Miedema manage in Arsenal's 11-1 win over Bristol City?**

a) Nine goals and one assist
b) Six goals and four assists
c) Three goals and seven assists
d) One goal and nine assists

**27. Why was the 1954 World Cup final so upsetting for Hungary?**

a) Their star player Ferenc Puskás had food poisoning and was sick on the pitch.
b) They lost 3–2 despite going 2–0 ahead.
c) The German referee disallowed three Hungary goals.
d) There was a kit clash so they played with bare chests.

**28. How did West Ham United assistant coach Harry Redknapp react to a fan shouting at him during a friendly match?**

a) He invited him to sit next to him in the dugout.
b) He poured a glass of cold water over his head.
c) He asked him to make the substitutions and followed his instructions.
d) He made him play the whole of the second half in attack.

**29. What type of penalty did Antonín Panenka invent?**

a) A slow chip down the middle of the goal
b) A blaster into the top corner
c) A strike that goes in after hitting both posts
d) A shot that hits the crossbar

**30. What was Garrincha best known for?**

a) Scoring from free kicks
b) Tackling
c) Dribbling
d) Farting

**31. Alphonso Davies and his family left a refugee camp in Ghana to settle in which country?**

a) Germany
b) USA
c) Canada
d) Mexico

**32. What message does USA defender Carson Pickett have tattooed on her right forearm?**

a) I love soccer
b) Family comes first
c) Be yourself
d) Imperfection is beauty

**33. What did Nikolai Starostin have to share with the son of Soviet leader Josef Stalin, apparently for his own safety?**

a) His toothbrush
b) His underwear
c) His bed
d) His football boots

**34. During the coronavirus pandemic, England striker Marcus Rashford helped raise £20 million to provide what for vulnerable schoolchildren?**

a) Free books
b) Free meals
c) Free calculators
d) Free shoes

**35. Why did Real Madrid end up paying such a high fee for teenager Vinícius Júnior?**

a) He is Pelé's grandson.
b) The Brazilian government added a tax on European teams signing their players.
c) Barcelona, who had just sold Neymar for a world record fee, were also trying to sign him.
d) He has two younger brothers they also hope to sign in the future.

36. **How did Cristiano Ronaldo help Portugal win the final of the 2016 European Championships?**

a) He scored a hat-trick.
b) He saved a penalty.
c) He was stretchered off but coached the team from the sidelines.
d) He gave everyone a foot massage before the game.

37. **What did Luke Matheson do one day after scoring against Manchester United at Old Trafford?**

a) Pass his driving test
b) Sit an exam as part of his A-Level studies
c) Sign a professional contract
d) Get a haircut

38. **What was the name of the spontaneous save that goalkeeper Rene Higuita made famous in a match against England?**

a) Scorpion Kick
b) Spider Punch
c) Lizard Leap
d) Kangaroo Kick

39. **How did Iran's shepherd-turned-goalkeeper Alireza Beiranvand get so good at throwing the ball long distances?**

a) His first sport was javelin.
b) He played a stone-throwing game when he was a boy.
c) He used to throw feed for sheep in distant fields.
d) He grew up on a diet of spinach.

40. **Christine Sinclair took 290 matches and 7,260 days to score a record 185 international goals for Canada. How many different teams did she score against?**

a) 21
b) 41
c) 61
d) 81

**41. Why did coach Marcelo Bielsa ask to see a young player who was fast asleep when he visited his house in the middle of the night?**

a) To listen to his breathing patterns
b) To check he didn't snore
c) To look at his legs
d) To see if he sucked his thumb

**42. What is the nickname of Abdelhak Nouri, the Ajax winger who spent three years in a coma?**

a) Orangie
b) Lemonie
c) Crazie
d) Appie

**43. What did Everton fan Mick Cullen wear when he walked 1,000 miles from John O'Groats to Lands End for charity?**

a) A pair of Everton swimming trunks
b) Liverpool socks
c) A pair of lederhosen
d) Nothing at all

**44. Who was Vicente Navarro, who is memorialized as a statue in the stands of Spanish club Valencia?**

a) A blind fan who went to every home game for over 30 years
b) The scorer of the winning goal when Valencia won the 1941 Spanish Cup
c) The man who founded the club in 1919
d) The vendor who sold world-famous tortillas during half-time for 50 years

**45. How did Colin Weir earn the money to buy the club he supported, Partick Thistle?**

a) He found gold buried on a beach.
b) He inherited it from his aristocratic parents.
c) He won the EuroMillions lottery.
d) He won Britain's Got Talent

46. **What was the name of the Thai team that was trapped in a cave for 17 days?**

a) Fantastic Beasts
b) Crazy Pigs
c) Mad Sheep
d) Wild Boars

47. **How did René Marić get discovered for his job as an assistant coach?**

a) He did freestyle tricks outside a training ground every day.
b) He was related to a German coach.
c) He wrote a tactics blog.
d) He used to make breakfast for the team owner.

48. **What did Auxerre coach Guy Roux ask local farmers to donate to help the club?**

a) Goats' cheese for the half-time snacks
b) Goats' dung for the pitches
c) Goats' milk for the tearoom
d) Goats' ears for luck

49. **What is the nickname of the Zambia national team?**

a) The Squirrels
b) Copper Bullets
c) Indomitable Lions
d) Harambee Stars

50. **What did Erling Haaland say after scoring nine goals in one match for Norway Under-19s?**

a) "I think I should have scored ten."
b) "I'm sorry for scoring so many goals."
c) "I was a bit lucky as I might have been offside for the sixth."
d) "I can't believe the coach subbed me off at half-time."

# QUIZ ANSWERS

1. b)
2. c)
3. d)
4. d)
5. a)
6. a)
7. a)
8. c)
9. b)
10. d)
11. c)
12. a)
13. c)
14. d)
15. d)
16. b)
17. d)
18. d)
19. d)
20. b)
21. c)
22. a)
23. a)
24. c)
25. a)
26. b)

**27.**b)

**28.**d)

**29.**a)

**30.**c)

**31.**c)

**32.**d)

**33.**c)

**34.**b)

**35.**c)

**36.**c)

**37.**b)

**38.**a)

**39.**b)

**40.**b)

**41.**c)

**42.**d)

**43.**a)

**44.**a)

**45.**c)

**46.**d)

**47.**c)

**48.**b)

**49.**b)

**50.**a)

WRITE ABOUT YOUR OWN EPIC HEROES

# T… TBALL TIMES

…ON Date: ........................................

## Headline: .......................................

### Strapline: .........................................

Article: ...................................................

.......................................................................

.......................................................................

.......................................................................

Above: ..........................

The GOAL

Date: ..............................

# HEADLINE: ..................................

## Strapline: ..................................

Article: ..................

........................

........................

........................

........................

........................

........................

........................

........................

........................

........................

Home - BOTN News ✕

backofthenet.co.uk/.......................................

News | Fixtures | Teams | Tables

# Headline: ..................................

Strapline: ...................................

Date:

..............

Article: ............................................

..........................................................

..........................................................

..........................................................

# FOOTBALL
MAGAZINE

Date:......

# Headline: ..............................

## Strapline: ..............................

Article: ........................................

....................................................

....................................................

....................................................

That was an epic read!
Heroes can come in so many different forms. Dragons, divers, dogs...
And great Danes, like the one who helped Liverpool with their throw-ins.
We also met a super Swede, an incredible Iranian, some magnificent Magyars, a mind-boggling Mexican, and lots of brilliant Brits.
Yes, we encountered glorious Gunners, fabulous Foxes, a happy-go-lucky Hammer and a rebel Red Devil.
We explored the world of condors, ants and scorpions.
Intere-STING!
And the Brazilian who played in seven World Cups.
She is brilli-ANT!
AB
BL

We discovered the secret behind Lionel Messi's greatness.
That was awe-inspi-RING RING!
And saw how Marcus Rashford campaigned for free school meals.
Incr-EDIBLE!
All our heroes have found themselves at the centre of remarkable stories.
Some by accident, some by design.
Here's something we didn't tell you before.
You too are at the centre of a remarkable story. The story of you!
We think that with passion, self-belief and courage, you can also make history.
You are at the beginning of an amazing adventure.
Make it epic, everyone!
AB
BL

# ACKNOWLEDGEMENTS

There are actually 51 epic heroes in this book. Our illustrator Spike Gerrell is the king of the canvas, the principal of the pencil, the sultan of the sketch. In short, he is the GIOAT - the Greatest Illustrator of All Time. Take a bow, Spike!

As always, the epic backroom staff at Walker Books encouraged and inspired us to deliver our best. Epic thanks to head coach Daisy Jellicoe, creative playmaker Laurelie Bazin and sporting director Denise Johnstone-Burt. Thanks also to Ellen Abernathy, Josh Alliston, Rosi Crawley, Jo Humphrey-Davis, Jill Kidson, Rebecca Oram and Ed Ripley.

High fives to our epic agents Rebecca Carter, Kirsty Gordon, Ellis Hazelgrove, David Luxton, Rebecca Winfield and Nick Walters.

We would also like to thank the following experts and friends who helped us along the way: Dan Davies, Thomas Grønnemark, Karel Haring, Kristian Jack, Behnam Jafarzadeh, Stuart James, Mitchell Kaye, René Marić, James Montague, Antonín Panenka, Darren Tulett. You are all heroes as well!

Finally, Ben would like to thank Annie, Clemmy and Bibi for their continued support and inspiration – and Buddy for his epic enthusiasm and waggy tail. Alex would like to thank Nat, Zak and Barnaby.

# ABOUT YOUR COACHES

Alex Bellos writes for the *Guardian.* He has written several bestselling popular science books and created two mathematical colouring books. He loves puzzles.

Ben Lyttleton is a journalist, broadcaster and football consultant. He has written books about how to score the perfect penalty and what we can learn from football's best managers.

Spike Gerrell grew up loving both playing football and drawing pictures. He now gets to draw for a living. At heart, though, he will always be a central midfielder.

COLLECT THE FOOTBALL SCHOOL SERIES
FOOTBALL SCHOOL
Season 1
WHERE FOOTBALL EXPLAINS RULES THE WORLD
FOOTBALL SCHOOL
Season 2
WHERE FOOTBALL EXPLAINS SAVES THE WORLD
ALEX BELLOS BEN LYTTLETON
FOOTBALL SCHOOL
Season 3
WHERE FOOTBALL EXPLAINS TACKLES THE WORLD
ALEX BELLOS
OVER 300 FAN-TASTIC QUESTIONS
FOOTBALL SCHOOL
THE AMAZING QUIZ BOOK
TEST YOUR WORLD CUP KNOWLEDGE!
ALEX BELLOS BEN LYTTLETON
FOOTBALL SCHOOL
Season 4
WHERE FOOTBALL EXPLAINS CELEBRATES THE WORLD
ALEX BELLOS BEN LYTTLETON
FOOTBALL SCHOOL
STAR PLAYERS
50 INSPIRING STORIES OF TRUE FOOTBALL HEROES
ALEX BELLOS BEN LYTTLETON
FOOTBALL SCHOOL
THE ULTIMATE PUZZLE BOOK
100 BRILLIANT BRAIN-TEASERS
ALEX BELLOS BEN LYTTLETON
OVER 200 SIDE-SPLITTING JOKES
FOOTBALL SCHOOL
THE INCREDIBLE JOKE BOOK
WHAT'S A STRIKER'S FAVOURITE MAGIC ROUTINE?
A HAT TRICK!
BEN LYTTLETON